The Girl Aviators And The Phantom Airship

by

Margaret Burnham

The Girl Aviators And The Phantom Airship
by Margaret Burnham

ISBN: 978-93-57481-79-3

Published by

DOUBLE 9 BOOKS

2/13-B, Ansari Road
Daryaganj, New Delhi – 110002
info@double9books.com
www.double9books.com
Tel. 011-40042856

ABOUT THE AUTHOR

The Girl Aviators' Motor Butterfly is one of the books by Margaret Burnham. Margaret Burnham was a novelist who lived from July 1884 to February 1971 and was born in Chicago, United States. She has worked on different books with his amazing thoughts, which resulted in The Girl Aviators and the Phantom Airship, The Girl Aviators' Sky Cruise, The Girl Aviators on Golden Wings, and The Girl Aviators Motor Butterfly. This collection of Fictional stories by Margaret Burnham attempts to compile many of his classic thoughts and offer them at an affordable price, by consolidating them into a single draft so that everyone can read them. Many of the books by Margaret Burnham have been out of print for decades and therefore have not been accessible to the general public. Most of her books belong to the Fictional genre.

CONTENTS

CHAPTER I.
THE GOLDEN BUTTERFLY.

"Roy! Roy! where are you?"

Peggy Prescott came flying down the red-brick path, a rustling newspaper clutched in her hand.

"Here I am, sis,—what's up?"

The door of a long, low shed at the farther end of the old-fashioned garden opened as a clattering sound of hammering abruptly ceased. Roy Prescott, a wavy-haired, blue-eyed lad of seventeen, or thereabouts, stood in the portal. He looked very business-like in his khaki trousers, blue shirt and rolled up sleeves. In his hand was a shiny hammer.

Peggy, quite regardless of a big, black smudge on her brother's face, threw her arms around his neck in one of her "bear hugs," while Roy, boy-like, wriggled in her clasp as best he could.

"Now, just look here," cried Peggy, quite out of breath with her own vehemence. She flourished the paper under his nose and, imitating the traditional voice of a town crier, announced:

"Hear ye! Hear ye! Hear ye! Roy Prescott or any of the ambitious aviators—now is your chance! Great news from the front! Third and last call!"

"You've got auctioneering, the Supreme Court and war times, mixed up a bit, haven't you?" asked Roy with masculine condescension, but gazing fondly at his vivacious sister nevertheless.

Peggy made a little face and then thrust forth the paper for his examination.

"Read that, you unenthusiastic person," she demanded, "and then tell me if you don't think that Miss Margaret Prescott has good reason to feel somewhat more enthusiastic than comports with her usual dignity and well-known icy reserve—ahem!"

"Good gracious, sis!" exclaimed the boy, as he scanned the news-sheet, "why this is just what we were wishing for, isn't it? It's our chance if we can only grasp it and make good."

"We can! We will!" exclaimed Peggy, striking an attitude and holding one hand above her glossy head. "Read it out, Roy, so that Monsieur Bleriot can hear it."

M. Bleriot, a French bull-dog, who had dignifiedly followed Peggy's mad career down the path, gazed up appreciatively, as Roy read out:

"Big Chance for Sky Boys!

"Ironmaster Higgins of Acatonick Offers Ten Thousand Dollars In Prizes for Flights and Planes."

"Ten thousand dollars, just think!" cried Peggy, clasping her hands one minute and the next stooping to caress M. Bleriot. "Oh, Roy! Do you think we could?"

"Could what? you indefinite person?" parried Roy, although his eyes were dancing and he knew well enough what his vivacious sister was driving at.

"Could win that ten thousand dollars, of course, you goose."

Roy laughed.

"It's not all offered in a lump sum," he rejoined. "Listen; there is a first prize of five thousand dollars for the boy under eighteen who makes the longest sustained flight in a plane of his own construction—with the exception of the engine, that is; and here's another of two thousand five hundred dollars to the glider making the best and longest sustained flight, and another of one thousand five hundred to the boy flying the most carefully constructed machine and the one bearing the most ingenious devices for perfecting the art of flying and—and—oh listen, Peggy!"

"I am—oh, I am!" breathed Peggy with half assumed breathlessness.

"There's a prize offered for girls!"

"No!"

"Yes. Now don't say any more that girls are downtrodden and neglected by the bright minds of the day. Here it is, all in black and white, a prize of a whole thousand to the young lady who makes a successful flight. There, what do you think of that?"

"That Mr. Higgins is a mean old thing," pouted Peggy, "five thousand dollars to the successful boy and only one thousand to the successful girl. It's discrimination, that's what it is. Don't you read every day in the papers about girls and women making almost as good flights as the men? Didn't a—a Mademoiselle somebody-or-other make a flight round the bell tower at Bruges the other day, and hasn't Col. Roosevelt's daughter been up in one, and isn't there a regular school for women fliers at Washington, and—and—?"

"Didn't the suffragettes promise to drop 'Votes for Women' placards from the air upon the devoted heads of the British Parliament, you up to date young person?" finished Roy, teasingly.

Peggy made a dash for him but the boy dodged into the shed, closely followed by his sister.

But as she crossed the threshold Peggy's wild swoop became a decorous stroll, so to speak. She paused, all out of breath, beneath a spreading expanse of yellow balloon silk, braced and strengthened with brightly gleaming wires and stays,—one wing of the big monoplane upon which her brother had spent all his spare time for the past year. The flying thing was almost completed now. It stood in its shed, with its scarab-like wings outspread like a newly alighted yellow butterfly, which, by a stroke of ill luck, had found itself installed in a gloomy cage instead of the bright, open spaces of its native element.

In one corner of the shed was a large crate surrounded by some smaller ones. The large one had been partially opened and Peggy gave a little squeal of delight as her eyes fell on it.

"Oh, Roy, that's it?"

"That's it," rejoined the boy proudly, lifting a bit of sacking from the contents of the opened crate, "isn't it a beauty?"

The lifted covering had exposed a gleam of bright, scarlet enamel, and the glint of polished brass. To Roy the contents of that crate was the splendid new motor for his aeroplane. But to Peggy, just then, it was something far different. A bit of a mist dimmed her shining eyes for an instant. Her voice grew very sober.

"Three thousand dollars—oh, Roy, it scares me!"

Roy crossed the shed and threw an arm about his sister's neck.

"Don't be frightened, sis," he breathed in an assuring tone, "it's going to be all right. Why, can't you see that the very first thing that happens is a chance to win $5,000?"

"I know that. But that contest is not to come off for more than a month and—and supposing someone should have a better machine than you?"

For an instant that air of absolute assurance, which truth to tell, had made Roy some enemies, and which was his greatest fault, left him. His face clouded and he looked troubled. But it was as momentary as the cloud-shadow that passes over a summer wheat field.

"It'll be all right, sis," he rejoined, confidently, "and if it isn't, I can always sell out to Simon Harding. You know he said that his offer held good at any time."

"I know that, Roy," rejoined Peggy, seriously, "but we could never do that. We could neither of us go against father's wishes like that. He—well, Roy, it's not to be thought of. Poor dad—"

Her bright eyes filled with tears as her mind travelled back to a scene of a year before when Mr. Prescott had ceased from troubling with the affairs of this world, and commended his children to the care of their maiden aunt—his sister with whom, since their mother's death some years before, the little family had made their home.

Poor Mr. Prescott had been that hopelessly impracticable creature—an inventor. Fortunately for himself, however, he had a small fortune of his own so that he had been enabled to carry on his dreaming and planning without embarrassing his family. Roy and Peggy had both been sent to good boarding schools, and had known, in fact, very little of home life after their mother's death which had occurred several years before, as already said.

Mr. Prescott, in his dreamy, abstract way, had cared dearly for his children. But those other children of his—the offsprings of his brain—that surrounded him in his workshop, had, somehow, seemed always to mean more to him. And so the young Prescotts had grown up without the benefit of home influences.

On Peggy's naturally sweet, vivacious character, this had not made so much difference. But Roy had developed, in spite of his real sterling worth and ability, into a headstrong, rather self-opinionated lad. His success at school in athletics and the studies which he cared about "mugging" at had not tended to decrease these qualities.

It had come as a shock to both of them a year before when two telegrams had been despatched—one to Peggy's school up the Hudson, and the other to Roy up in Connecticut, telling them to return to the Long Island village of Sandy Bay at once. Their father—that half-shadowy being—was very ill.

The messages had not exaggerated the seriousness of the situation. Three days after his children reached his side Mr. Prescott gently breathed his last, dying, as he had lived, so quietly, that the end had come before they realized it. But in those last brief moments Roy came to know his father better than ever before. He learned that the dream of his parent had been to produce an aeroplane free from the defects of its forerunners,—a safe vehicle for passengers or freight. How far he had progressed in this there was no time for him to tell before the end came. But Roy, interested already in aeronautics at school, where he had been president of "The High Fliers"—a model aeroplane association,—eagerly took up his father's desire that he would try to carry on his work, and began to take lessons in flying.

In the shed which had been Mr. Prescott's workshop the framework of an aeroplane already stood. And with the aid of what money his father had left him, Roy had carried on the work till now it was almost completed. But the three thousand dollars which had gone for the motor had completely exhausted the lad's legacy. As Peggy put it, all their eggs were in an "aerial basket."

But how much Peggy had aided him, in what had, in the last few months possessed all his thoughts, Roy did not guess. To what extent her encouragement had spurred him on to surmount seemingly unconquerable difficulties, and how she had actually aided him in constructing the machine, his ambition never realized. Not innately selfish, Roy was yet too used to having his own way to attribute his success to any one but himself.

Sometimes, brave, loyal little Peggy, try as she might, could not disguise this from herself, and it pained her a good deal. But she had uncomplainingly, ungrudgingly, aided her brother, without hoping for, or expecting, the appreciation she sometimes felt she was really entitled to. But her great love for her brother kept Peggy from ever betraying to him or any one else an iota of her inner feelings.

So intent had the brother and sister been on their talk that neither of them had noticed, while they conversed, that a big four-door touring car, aglitter with gleaming maroon paint, and with a long, low hood concealing a powerful engine, had glided up to the white gate in the picket fence surrounding Miss Prescott's old fashioned cottage.

From it a frank, pleasant-faced lad and an unusually striking girl, tall, slender and with a glossy mass of black hair coiled attractively on her shapely head, had alighted.

Hearing the sound of voices from the open door of the shed in which The Golden Butterfly, as Peggy had christened it, was nearing completion, they, without ceremony, at once made their way toward it. Peggy, glancing up from her sad reverie at the sound of footsteps, gave a glad little cry as she beheld the visitors standing framed in the sunlight of the open door. While she and the tall, dark-haired girl mingled their contrasting tresses in an exuberant school-girl caress, the lad and Roy Prescott, were, boy fashion, slapping one another on the back and shaking hands with just as much enthusiasm.

"Why, if this isn't simply delightful, Jess, you dear old thing," cried the delighted Peggy, as, with both hands on her chum's shoulders, she held Jess Bancroft off at arm's length, the better to scrutinize her handsome face, "and Jimsy, too," as she turned to the lad with a bright smile of welcome; "wherever did you two come from?"

"From the clouds?" demanded Roy.

"No, hardly, although I don't wonder at your asking such a question," laughed Jess, merrily, exchanging greetings with Roy. "Roy Prescott, positively I can see your wings sprouting."

They all laughed heartily at this, while Jess ran on to explain that she and her brother were stopping for the summer at Seaview Towers, a summer estate which their father, a Wall Street power, had leased for the season. Of course, explained the merry girl, who had been Peggy's closest chum at school, her first thought had been to take a spin over in her new motor car and look up her friends, for Roy and James—or Jimsy—Bancroft had been almost as close chums as the girls.

"And so this is the wonderful Golden Butterfly that you wrote to me about?" exclaimed Jess enthusiastically after the first buzz of conversation subsided.

"Yes, this is it," said Roy with great satisfaction in his tones, "and I'm proud of it, I can tell you. I think I've made a success of it."

Jess and Jimsy exchanged glances. And then Jess stole a look at Peggy, but no cloud had crossed the face of Roy's sister.

"Oh, you darling," thought Jess, "you're too sweet for anything. I just know how much you contributed to the Golden Butterfly's existence, and yet you won't detract a bit from Roy's self satisfaction."

As for Jimsy Bancroft, he said nothing. He glanced rather oddly at Roy for an instant. Then his eyes turned to Peggy's face. Perhaps they dwelt there for rather a long period of time. At any rate, they were still fixed on her brave beauty when a sudden shadow fell across the stream of sunlight that poured into the open portal of the workshop.

"Ah! So this is the place in which young genius finds its habitation;" grated out a rather harsh, unpleasant voice.

They all looked up. Perhaps none of them—Jimsy least of all—was pleased at the interruption. The newcomer was a tall, angular man, with a withered, clean-shaven face,—what Peggy called a "money making face"; and surely that described Simon Harding, as he stood there in his black, none-too-new garments, and his square-toed shoes. One could fairly catch the avaricious glint in his eyes as he squinted rapidly over the new aeroplane's outlines.

By his side stood a youth who was, so far as dress went at any rate, the exact opposite of the elder man. Fanning Harding—or Fan as he was usually called—was dressed in elaborate motoring costume. His goggles, of the latest and most exaggerated design, were shoved up off his countenance now, exposing to view a good-looking browned face. It was marred, however, by the same restless, strained look that could be seen on his father's visage.

"We're not intruding, I hope," he hastened to say, coming forward with a cordiality that seemed somewhat forced.

"Not in the least," said Peggy, hastily, realizing that none of them had perhaps looked very cordial, "won't you come in?"

Fan Harding, bestowing an admiring glance on her, seemed to be about to accept. His father, however, struck in:

"I'll leave you with the young folks, my boy, while I go up to the house. I have some business with Miss Prescott."

As he shuffled off, Peggy and Roy exchanged somewhat uneasy glances. What business could this old man—in some respects a power financially and otherwise in Sandy Beach—have with their aunt?

"Say Peggy," spoke up Fan Harding, suddenly, "ain't you going to introduce me to your friends? And how about inviting us all to have some of those strawberries Pop and I noticed as we came down the path?"

"Well, he isn't a bit backward about coming forward!" thought Jess as the young people, with due formality, went through the ceremony of introductions.

CHAPTER II.
SUSPENSE AND ACHIEVEMENT.

It was a week after Fan Harding's visit to the Prescott home, on one windless, steamy morning, when the pearl-gray mist still lay in the smooth hollows running back from the coast, that The Golden Butterfly was wheeled out of her cocoon—so to speak—and dragged up the hillside at the back of the white, green-shuttered cottage. Miss Prescott, a sweet-faced old lady, whose cheek was still blooming despite the passage of the years, stood on the back porch of the house watching the process.

If Miss Prescott's face had been somewhat less cheerful than usual since her talk with Mr. Harding, all the clouds had been chased from it now. She watched as eagerly as a girl while Roy and Peggy, aided by Jess and Jimsy and two other lads, friends of Roy's from the village, dragged the brand new aeroplane up the hillside.

The excited chatter and laughter of the young folks rang out merrily as they worked—for it was work to get the 'plane, light as it was, up the grade. Fortunately—for Roy had no desire of a crowd to witness his initial ascent in the new 'plane—the Prescott house was some distance out of the village, and there were no near neighbors. The place had, in fact, once been a farm house, and although the acreage still was in the possession of Miss Prescott it was not worked.

A more ideal place for flying could not be imagined. Smooth slopes—unwooded, except in clumps—were all about. To the north glimmered the sparkling waters of Long Island Sound, while to the south stretched fertile farming land, devoted to crop-raising and pasturage.

Very business-like the young people looked as they hauled the monoplane up the hill. Roy and Jimsy wore leather puttees, trousers fashioned somewhat like riding breeches, and leather coats. On their heads were caps of the latter material, well padded within and provided with visors pierced with goggles.

The girls wore shirt waists, outing skirts and "sensible" walking boots. Jess had on her "Shaker" motoring bonnet, in which she looked very captivating indeed. Peggy's glossy hair, unadorned, but tightly confined in a net, formed her hair covering. Both girls were all a-tiptoe with excitement, for although Roy had had experience with aeroplanes, and so, in a limited way, had Jimsy, this feature of the sport was new to them.

At last the summit was reached, and Roy, after calling a halt, took a brief but comprehensive survey of the Golden Butterfly. This done, he climbed into the chassis—or body—of the thing, and leaning over the machinery he rapidly tested all the adjustments and examined the lubricating devices to see that all was in order. Everything appeared to be.

"Well," said Roy, with some self complacency, stepping out of the machine, "everything seems to be ready for the initial flight of the Golden Butterfly, my lords and gentlemen."

"And ladies, if you please," put in Jess, in a voice that was vibrant with excitement, despite her endeavor to keep calm.

"And ladies," added Roy, with a gallant bow in her direction.

Peggy in the meantime, like an anxious little mother fussing over dolls, had been examining the aeroplane once more. Suddenly she gave a little cry. The exclamation interrupted Roy who was explaining, with great satisfaction, that everything was all right.

"I've looked it over and if there had been anything wrong it couldn't have escaped my notice," he observed rather pompously.

"Oh, Roy! Just look here! The spring of this landing wheel is all slack!"

This was the exclamation from Peggy that brought up Roy somewhat shortly in the midst of his self-confident harangue.

"By George, so it is, sis!" exclaimed Roy, reddening a little, while Lem Sidney, one of his chums, observed with a chuckle to Jeff Stokes, that Peggy appeared to know as much, if not more, about the machine than did Roy.

The spring was soon tightened by means of a monkey wrench. But that did not prevent them all realizing that had it not been for Peggy's acute observation a serious accident might have occurred. This done, even Peggy's anxious glances could not detect any other flaw in the machine.

"What time did that aviator fellow say he would show up?" then demanded Jimsy, abruptly.

"He should be here now," rejoined Roy. "I've half a mind to start anyhow. I can manage the machine I am very certain."

"Oh, Roy!" cried Peggy, reprovingly, "you know you promised aunty that you wouldn't do anything till Mr. Hal Homer got here."

"All right, sis," put in Roy, hastily, "don't be scared. I'll stick to my word."

"Hullo!" cried Jimsy, suddenly, "there comes an auto now."

"So it is," exclaimed the others, as a black touring car came whizzing down the road below them. It soon halted, and a figure in leather garments with gaitered legs alighted and hastened across the fields toward the party clustered about the aeroplane. The car was left in charge of the chauffeur.

As Jimsy had guessed, the new arrival proved to be Hal Homer, the well-known cross country flier, from whom Roy had taken some vacation time aviation lessons.

"He's awfully good looking," whispered Jess to Peggy, after introductions to the dapper young aviator had been extended by Roy.

"Oh, so—so," rejoined Peggy, with a toss of her head.

"Maybe you know some one who is handsomer?" questioned Jess with a mischievous side glance of her fine eyes.

Peggy flushed under her fair skin. But Jess laughed with good-humored raillery.

"Jimsy surely is a good-looking boy," she said, "if he hadn't a pug nose."

"A pug nose!" flared up Peggy. "Oh, Jess, how can—"

Then she stopped short in confusion while Jess laughed the more at her discomfiture.

Young Mr. Homer lost no time in starting operations. He ordered his helpers to secure the machine to a small tree growing nearby by means of a stout rope Roy had brought with him. This done, and the monoplane thus secured from flying away when her engine was started, he set the sparking and gasolene levers and threw in the switch. Roy and Jimsy, the latter acting under Roy's instructions, flew to the propeller.

The Golden Butterfly being a monoplane, this was in front of the machine.

"Be careful when you feel it start, to leap aside," warned Roy, "or you might be beheaded."

"I never lose my head in an emergency," joked Jimsy.

But just the same his heart beat, as did those of all of them but Hal Homer's, as he and Roy started to swing the great shiny wooden driving appliance.

Once, twice, three times they swung it round, exerting all their force. The fourth time they were rewarded by a feeble sigh from the engine—a sixty horse power motor.

All at once—Bang!

"Let go!" yelled Roy, jumping backward.

Jimsy in his hurry to obey stumbled and fell backward in a heap. He rolled some distance down the hill unnoticed, before he succeeded in stopping his motion. In the meantime the others—even Peggy—were too absorbed in the sight before them to watch Jimsy.

Simultaneously with the sharp report the propeller had whirled around swiftly. The next instant it was a mere gray blur, while a furious wind from its revolving blades swept the onlookers. Blue smoke spurted from the exhausts, mingled with flame, and the uproar was terrific.

The Golden Butterfly, like a thing of life, struggled at her moorings. The rope stretched and strained, taut as a violin string, under the pull. But it held fast, and after a while Aviator Homer slowed down the engine and finally stopped it, after adjusting a miss-fire in one of the cylinders. As the propeller became once more visible and then came to a stop, the boys broke into cheers, while the girls, too, voiced their enthusiasm.

"Oh, Peggy, isn't it a darling!" cried Jess.

"Aeroplanes are not usually called 'darlings,'" responded Peggy with assumed severity, "but—oh, Jess, it's—it's—a jewel and—"

"I'm dying for a ride in it!" burst in Jess.

"Then if you will consent to live a little longer I hope to have the pleasure of saving your life," put in Roy, gallantly.

"Oh, Roy! I can ride in it now!" gasped Jess, while Peggy clasped her hands and snuggled up close to her chum.

"Well, no, hardly just yet," laughed Roy, "but after Homer has tested her thoroughly out I guess you girls can take a spin."

"You know I'm going to learn to handle one," declared Peggy, as Roy made off once more. "I know a good deal about the theoretical part of it already."

"Well, theory wouldn't do you much good in a mile-long tumble," quoth Jess, sagely.

"Nonsense," rejoined Peggy. "Mr. Homer says one is as safe in an aeroplane, if one is careful, as in an auto."

"Safer I guess, the way that brother of mine drives sometimes," replied Jess. "He calls it 'burning up the road.' But—oh, look, they're casting off, or whatever it is you do to an airship when you turn her loose. Oh!"

Snatching off her motoring bonnet Jess began waving it furiously. While they had been talking the rope had been cast loose, and now, with Mr. Homer himself at the driving wheel, in cap and goggles, the engine was being started once more.

In wrapt excitement both girls stood breathless. So intent were they on the scene transpiring before them that they had not noticed the approach of a second auto on the road below. From it Fan Harding had alighted and hastened up the hill, after "parking" his machine, as if in fear that he would be too late to view the proceedings.

A sneering look was on his rather handsome face as he rapidly climbed the hill. He reached a position behind the two girls just as the aviator gave the signal to let go of the machine—to the rear structure of which Lem Sidney and Jeff Stokes were perspiringly clinging, their heels digging into the soft turf to steady themselves.

As Mr. Homer's hand swung backward and downward they let go. Instantly, like an arrow from a bow, the monoplane—the work of Peggy and Roy—was off. How it scudded across the hill top! Blue smoke and flame shot from its exhaust. Its operator sat hunched over his machinery looking, with his goggles, like some creature of the lower regions. Peggy clasped her hands and stood a-tiptoe breathlessly as it scudded along.

"Oh, will it rise?" she breathed, her color coming and going in her excitement.

"I'll bet ten dollars it won't fly any more than an earthworm."

Peggy turned swiftly, indignantly. Her color flamed and her eyes blazed angrily. Jess, hardly less indignant at the sneering tone and words, also faced about.

"Good morning, girls," said Fan Harding, easily, raising his motoring cap nonchalantly, "I came to see the ascension, but I'm afraid that it's going to be a descension."

"I think you're hateful to talk like that," cried Peggy, angrily, stamping her foot. "Our aeroplane will rise. It just will, I tell you—oh, gracious!"

She broke off in confusion and stood aghast for a moment. The swiftly scudding aeroplane had stopped its skittering over the grass and had come to an abrupt stop at a distance of about five hundred yards.

Already the boys were running across the turf toward it at top speed. The girls could see Mr. Homer clambering out of the chassis as the machine came to a standstill.

"Ha! Ha! just as I thought," chuckled Fan Harding, viciously, "that thing is a dead failure."

Poor Peggy, tears in her eyes at this seeming disaster, was stung fairly out of herself. She switched round on Fan Harding with a suddenness that made her skirt fly out and that young gentleman step precipitately backward.

"It isn't a failure, Fan Harding," she cried, with blazing eyes. "How dare you come here to sneer at us. We didn't invite you. Oh, I could—"

But Jess had seized her arm and succeeded in checking Peggy just in time. She whispered something to the indignant girl, who, with a scornful look at Fan Harding, turned and, with her friend, ran lightly off toward the stranded aeroplane.

"By Jove, I really thought for a minute she was going to slap my face," chuckled Fan Harding to himself. "How pretty she is when she is angry. But I guess if she knew what I do about certain affairs she wouldn't be quite so fresh with me."

He cast a glance at the aeroplane around which the anxious young people were now clustering thickly.

"If that thing is a success," he mused, as he strode off to join them, "so much the better for me. I think I could use an aeroplane. I don't see why I should let Roy Prescott beat me out at anything. Ah! They've started the engine again and—by ginger, she's rising! She's going up! She's flying!"

The small irregularity in the working of the engine, which had brought the plane to a stop, had been quickly remedied. Even Fan Harding, little as he liked Roy, could not help but join in the cheers as the Golden Butterfly, swinging in an easy circle, began to climb— higher and higher toward the fleecy clouds that flecked the blue dome above.

As for Peggy, she jumped up and down in her enthusiasm till her golden hair was tumbling in a tangle about her pink shells of ears.

"Oh, goody! goody! goody!" she squealed in the intensity of her joy.

CHAPTER III.
THE CLOUDS GATHER.

"And so unless we can raise that money somehow within a short time we shall have to leave dear old Shadyside!"

It was Roy who spoke, in troubled tones, some days after the successful flight of the Golden Butterfly. They were seated in the cool-looking living room of Miss Prescott's home. The sun filtering in through the Venetian blinds, fell in patches on the polished floors—Peggy's work, for Miss Prescott's circumstances had been for some time too straitened to afford the servants she formerly had. But she had kept all knowledge of her struggle from her nephew and niece, until now the time had arrived when she felt that she could conceal no longer the object of old Sam Harding's visit to her.

The old man, among other things, was President of the Sandy Bay Bank. This bank, although the children did not know it, had long held a mortgage on Miss Prescott's property. The kindly, sweet-souled lady had incurred the debt to forward her brother's dreams. For poor Mr. Prescott had always been "just on the verge of making a fortune." Mr. Harding's errand was to state that the interest being long overdue and there being no immediate prospect of settlement the bank would have to foreclose. The real reason for this anxiety, which of course Miss Prescott, simple-minded lady, could not know, was, that a real estate concern wanted to purchase the property to erect a summer colony.

"But what of my securities in—and—and—?" inquired poor Miss Prescott, who really knew no more of business than Peggy's French bull-dog.

"In the depressed state of the market that class of securities are worth nothing, madam," was the response, "in addition, though I have refrained from telling you so till now, your account at the bank is much overdrawn. However," he had continued, "to show you that we mean to be fair with you we will say nothing about that, but unless the bank gets its interest we must have the land."

It was Miss Prescott's relation of the true state of affairs to Roy and Peggy that sunny afternoon that had brought forth Roy's exclamation recorded at the beginning of this chapter.

"But, auntie," burst out Peggy, blankly, "does the man mean to say that there is nothing, absolutely nothing, on which we can realize anything?"

Miss Prescott shook her head slowly.

"There is nothing we can do," she rejoined, sadly. "We shall have to leave dear old Shadyside and the land will be cut up and sold to strangers. Land which the first Prescott settled on and which has been in the family ever since. Oh, dear!" and Miss Prescott, never the most strong-minded of women, drew out her handkerchief and began to sniff ominously. Peggy, looking bewitchingly pretty in a simple muslin frock, wrinkled her forehead seriously.

"It can't—it simply can't be as bad as all that," she persisted. "We can raise the money somehow."

"Five thousand dollars!" cried Miss Prescott.

"Phew! That is a lot of money," from Roy. But Peggy had jumped up from her chair.

"The contest, Roy! The contest!" she was exclaiming. "We must write this very day for particulars. If the Golden Butterfly can win that prize—"

"By Jove, sis, it's five thousand dollars, isn't it?" burst out Roy, almost equally excited. "I'd forgotten all about it up till now. What an idiot I am. If only—"

He stopped short suddenly, struck by a depressing thought. Probably there were plenty of machines, most of them far better than the Golden Butterfly, entered in the contest which they had read about. His enthusiasm died away—as was the way with Roy—almost as quickly as it had flamed up.

But Peggy would not hear of hesitation. She made Roy sit down that very night and write to the committee in charge of the Higgins' prize. Under her brave, independent urgings things began to look brighter. It was a fairly cheerful party that sat down to a simple supper that evening.

"Oh, dear," sighed Peggy, in the course of the meal, "if only I knew some one who needed a bright young woman to run an aeroplane, how I'd jump at the job."

"You ought to get a high salary at it anyhow," rather dolefully joked Roy.

"And make a high jump, too," laughed Peggy; "but seriously, auntie, I can run the Butterfly almost as well as Roy. Mr. Homer said so before he left. He said: 'Well, Miss Prescott, I've taught you all I know about an aeroplane. The rest lies with you, of course.'" Peggy went on modestly: "I could run an auto before. I learned on the one that Jess had at school, so it really wasn't hard to get to understand the engine. Don't you think I'm almost as good a—" Peggy paused for a word—"a—sky pilot!" she cried triumphantly, "as good a sky pilot as you are, Roy?"

"Almost," modestly admitted Roy, his mouth full of strawberry shortcake, "but never mind about that now, sis. There are more important things to be thought of than that. I'm going into town to-morrow for two things. One is to see Mr. Harding myself. It takes a man to tackle these things—"

"Oh, dear!" sniffed Peggy.

"The other bit of business I have to attend to," went on Roy, "is to get a position. It's time I was a breadwinner." Roy thought that sounded rather well and went on—"a breadwinner."

"Oh, Roy!" cried his aunt, admiringly, "do you think you'll be able to get a position?"

"Without a doubt, aunt," rejoined Roy, confidently; "no doubt several business houses would be glad—to have me with them," Roy was going to say but he thought better of it and concluded, "to give me a chance."

Peggy said nothing, which rather irritated the boy. He concluded, however, that being a girl, she could hardly be expected to appreciate the responsibilities of the man of the household. For since that afternoon and its disclosures, Roy had, in his own mind, assumed that important position.

Somewhat to Roy's surprise he found no difficulty in obtaining access to Mr. Harding at the bank. On the contrary, had he been expected he could not have been ushered into the old man's presence with greater promptness. He stated his business briefly and straightforwardly.

"Now, Mr. Harding," he concluded, "is there no way in which this matter can be straightened out?"

The old man, in the rusty black suit, picked up a pen and began drawing scrawly diagrams on the blotter in front of him. Apparently he was in deep thought. But had Roy been able to penetrate that mask-like face he would have been startled at what was passing in Simon Harding's mind. At last he spoke:

"I understand that you have built an aeroplane which is a success?" he questioned.

"That's right, sir," said Roy, flushing proudly; "but the ideas we put into it were my father's—every one of them. He practically made it his life work, you see, and—"

"And you beggared yourself carrying those ideas out, eh?" snarled the old man. "Oh, you need not look astonished. I know all about your affairs. More than you think for. And now having expended a wicked sum for the engine of this flying thing where do you expect to reap your profit?"

Roy was rather taken aback. In the past days—since the first wonderful flight of the Golden Butterfly—he had not given much thought to that part of it. He realized this now with a rather embarrassed feeling. Old Harding eyed him keenly.

"Why—father, before he died, spoke of the government, sir. He wanted the United States to have the benefit of the machine if it proved successful."

"Bah!" sneered old Harding, scornfully, "a mere visionary dream of an inventor. Now I have a business proposition to make to you. I myself am interested in aeroplanes—or rather in their manufacture."

"You, Mr. Harding!" Roy looked his astonishment. The last vehicle in the world one would have thought of in connection with "Old Money Grubber," as he was sometimes called, was an aeroplane. If he had been given to such things Roy would have concluded the old man was joking.

"Yes, sir," snapped Mr. Harding, "I am. But not directly. It's on Fanning's account. He tells me that he has a chance to organize a company to give aeroplane exhibitions and also to manufacture them. But he has not been able to find a suitable machine, or one that was not fully covered by patents till he saw yours in flight the other day."

Suddenly he raised his voice:

"Fanning! Come here a minute."

Almost immediately, through a door which Roy had not hitherto noticed, but which evidently led into an adjoining office, the figure of Simon Harding's son appeared. To his chagrin, Roy realized that almost every word he had said to the father must have been overheard by the son.

Young Harding, who was dressed in a flashy gray suit, with trousers rolled up very high to exhibit electric blue socks of the same hue as his necktie, greeted Roy, who felt suddenly very shabby and insignificant, with a patronizing nod.

"Sorry you're in difficulties, Roy," he said, "but you never were a business chap even at school."

The memory of certain monetary transactions in which young Harding had been concerned occurred to Roy. The other's patronizing air angered him. He would have liked to make some sharp, meaning retort. But the thought of Peggy and his aunt restrained him. Roy was beginning to learn fast.

"You needn't bother to tell me anything about the case," went on the younger Harding. "I accidentally overheard all that you said. Now, Roy, my father has stated the case to you correctly. I've got a chance to make money with aeroplanes if I can only get hold of a new model. You've got just what I want."

"Come to the point, my boy, come to the point," urged his father.

"I'm getting there, ain't I?" snarled the dutiful son. "Well, Roy, you're in pretty tight straits. We can foreclose on that mortgage any day we want to. But we won't do it if you give us a square deal. Forget the government. Make a deal with us consigning to me the right to manufacture and exhibit those aeroplanes and I'll set aside that mortgage and give you a thousand dollars to boot."

"And suppose I won't accept that offer?" asked Roy, slowly.

"Then we shall have to go ahead and foreclose. We want that land anyhow, but I am even more anxious to set up my son in a paying business," exclaimed old Harding. "Our offer is a fair one. It amounts to giving you six thousand dollars for a thing of canvas, wire and clockwork."

"Rather more than that, sir," said Roy, in a steady voice, although he was inwardly blazing.

"Well, what do you say?" asked Fanning, eagerly. "We'll draw up the papers right now if you say so."

But Roy was learning fast. He knew that the offer just made him had been an inadequate one.

"I'd like to have time to think it over," he said, hesitatingly.

"Take all the time you want," said old Harding, with a wave of his shrivelled, claw-like hand.

But Fanning did not seem so pleased. It flashed across his mind that Roy wanted to consult with Peggy, and somehow Fanning felt that in that case his offer would meet with refusal. He therefore resolved to put in a heavy blow.

"But I want to start at once," he said. "I can't wait any length of time. When you think that if you don't accept my offer you'll all be without a roof over your heads I should think that for the sake of your sister and your aunt you'd accept."

"They'll never be in that position while I can work," rejoined Roy, with a flushed face. He rose and picked up his hat. Somehow he felt that he could not stand Fanning very many minutes more.

"Yes, very fine talk, but what can you do?" snarled Simon Harding.

CHAPTER IV.
JESS AND ROY.

Roy flung back some sort of answer and hastened out of the office. As he made his way up the sunny street outside, however, he could not get out of his mind the words of Simon Harding. After all, they were true; "what could he do?" Mentally, as he walked along, Roy ran over the list of his accomplishments. He came to the conclusion that aeroplane building and flying was where his greatest strength lay. But how was he to proceed to make money with his knowledge?

At this point in his meditations, when, unnoticed, he had almost reached the end of the elm-shaded village street, a loud "Honk! Honk!" suddenly startled him.

He looked up, and his gloom vanished like a summer cloud as he saw smiling down on him from the driver's seat of the big auto which had just rolled up beside him, the sunny countenance of Jess Prescott. She was in automobile attire and looked unusually attractive.

"Oh, I am so glad I've run across you," she exclaimed.

"You almost did," laughed Roy.

"Did what?"

"Run across me, of course," was the response. "But what are you doing in town? And driving your own car, too. Where is Jimsy?"

"Oh, he had to do an errand for father."

"And so you are acting as chauffeur?"

"Yes, don't I make a nice one?"

"You certainly do," rejoined the lad with a great deal of emphasis.

"Well, that being the case, you are commanded to jump in by me at once. I've got an errand or two to do and then I'm driving home. We'll go by your place and I can drop you there."

"That's very good of you——" began Roy, but Jess cut him short.

"It's really selfish," she exclaimed. "I was looking for an escort. I really need one. You haven't got a revolver with you, have you?"

"Good gracious," exclaimed the astonished boy as he climbed into the big car; "no, of course not. Whatever do you want one for?"

"Why," confided Jess, as they sped along, "I'm on my way to the bank. Mother is going to a big dinner party to-night and I volunteered to fetch out her jewels for her from the safe deposit vault where she keeps them."

"And you were afraid of robbers holding you up?"

"Of course not," laughed the girl, skillfully dodging a vagrant dog that sped across the road in front of the big car; "but just the same, I'm glad to have a nice big boy like you with me. You see, some of the jewels are very valuable, and one never knows what might happen."

"No," agreed Roy; "but in broad daylight, on the road between Sandy Bay and your home, there could hardly be any risk. For instance, who would know that you had valuables in the car?"

"Nobody, except some of the servants at home probably," responded Jess. "But here's the bank."

As she spoke she skillfully manipulated her levers and pedals and brought the car to a stop against the curb as neatly as any driver could have accomplished it.

The car had hardly come to a stop before the bank door flew open and Fanning Harding emerged, his features drawn up into what he meant to be a pleasing smile, but which more resembled a smirk.

Jess, ignoring his proffered hand, leaped lightly to the sidewalk and, responding somewhat frigidly to his pleasantries, made her way into the bank. A cold nod was all that had passed between Fanning and Roy, though young Harding had looked astonished at beholding the other in Jess's car. Before long the girl tripped out of the building once more. But this time she carried with her a black leather case. Fanning was once more at her side and insisted on helping her into the car, holding her arm rather tightly as he did so.

"I wish I could accompany you," he said. "Ten thousand dollars' worth of jewels is a rather risky thing to carry about."

"Oh, I have a splendid escort, thank you," spoke up Jess, frigidly. She drew on her gauntlets and began fumbling with the levers. Roy was already out of the car and cranking up.

"It would be the pleasure of the ride," said Fanning, in a low voice. "If I were with you I could almost wish somebody would try to hold us up so that I could show you what I could do in your defence."

"Just as you did that day at school when poor little Henry Willis was being beaten by that big bully Hank Jones?" asked Jess, quietly. Fanning's glances, and the emphasis he threw into what he said, were very distasteful to her, and she took what proved an effectual means of squelching him.

"You know I had a sore wrist that day and couldn't get into a fight with Hank," said Fanning, but his eyes were downcast and he had not much more to say. Presently the auto chugged off, leaving the disgruntled youth standing on the sidewalk following it with his eyes.

"So you're trying to win out Jess Bancroft, are you?" the over-dressed lad thought to himself. "Well, Roy Prescott, I guess that settles you. I've never liked you, and now that I've a chance to get the upper hand of you I'm going to use it. You'll regret this auto ride to-day in days to come, or I'm very much mistaken."

He turned and reëntered the bank, but presently emerged again in a leather coat of black material, black leggings and black cap and goggles. Hauling out his motor-cycle from a rack in front of the bank he wheeled it into the street, and with an admiring crowd of small boys looking on, started the swift, four-cylindered machine. In a cloud of dust he vanished in the same direction as had Jess Bancroft's car.

Jess, once the confines of the village were past, "let the car out." They sped along, chatting merrily. The roads about Sandy Bay were ideal for automobiling, and perhaps neither of the young occupants of the car noticed how fast they were going when the vehicle topped a small rise and began descending a long steep grade at the bottom of which the railroad, which approached on a curve, was visible in two shining parallel streaks of metal.

Suddenly there came a shrill, long drawn whistle.

"Hullo, a train!" exclaimed Roy. "Must be a freight; there's no regular passenger scheduled to run at this time of day."

"That's right," agreed Jess. "I guess I'll slow down a bit till we see how close it is to the crossing."

She pressed her foot on the brake pedal and shoved hard.

But to her astonishment there was no diminution in the speed of the car. It plunged forward down the hill, gaining impetus every second.

"Better slow up, Jess," warned Roy, who had not noticed the girl grow white and faint, as the possibility of what might occur if she could not control the car flashed before her.

"I—I can't!" she gasped.

"The emergency brake!" almost shouted Roy. Below them he had seen a swiftly moving column of white smoke. It was the approaching train. Now it whistled once more. That meant it was close upon the crossing toward which the car was racing at terrific speed.

"I've—I've tried it. It's jammed or something! Oh, Roy! the train!"

Before she could say any more Roy had risen from his seat, and gently, but firmly, removed the girl's trembling hands from the steering wheel. With might and main he tried to check the car. But all he did was in vain. Drops of perspiration stood out upon his forehead. Jess, utterly unnerved, sank back in her seat and hid her face with her gloved hands.

Above the roar of the on-dashing car could be heard the sharp puffing of the approaching locomotive. Roy tugged as if he would tear his muscle out at the brake lever, but it refused to budge. A sort of desperate coolness came over him. But Jess, who had uncovered her eyes for an instant, gave a sudden shrill scream.

"Oh, we'll be killed! Look,—the train! We'll crash into it!"

"Sit down, Jess," ordered Roy, sternly, for the excited girl had seemed to be on the point of jumping from the car as it swayed and bumped toward what seemed certain annihilation, at a terrific rate.

Roy glanced desperately about him. The hill was enclosed by steepish banks with hedgerows at the top. But at one point he thought he saw a chance of escape.

As he despairingly changed the direction of the car two figures sprang from behind the hedge and gazed in amazement at the runaway auto.

"They'll be killed to a certainty!" cried one.

Indeed it seemed so. With Jess in a dead faint and Roy looking straight into the dark face of danger the uncontrolled car tore onward toward the train. The engineer saw it now and blew his whistle shrilly.

CHAPTER V.
A NARROW ESCAPE.

But Roy's quick eye had noted one loophole of escape,—a gap in the bank.

Truly it was taking a terrible risk to dash the car through it. The boy did not know what lay beyond, and in taking the chance he was running almost as great a risk of annihilation as if he kept straight on. But to have done the latter would have been to crash into a solid wall of moving freight cars as they bumped across the grade crossing.

It was almost certain that they would be thrown out and maybe injured. But Roy did not hesitate. With a quick twist of his steering wheel he sent the car spinning on two wheels for the gap. For an instant it seemed as if the vehicle would capsize under the sudden change of direction. But it did not, although it tilted over at a dangerous angle.

Whiz-z-z-z-z!

In a flash they were through the gap, the landscape blurring, so terrific was the speed.

The next instant there was a sickening shock. Instinctively Roy threw out an arm to protect his fair companion. Hardly had he done so before he felt himself impelled through the air as if from a catapult, and all grew blank.

When Roy came to himself his head ached as if it would burst. It was some few seconds, in fact, before he realized what had occurred. When he did he looked about him. A few paces away lay the still form of Jess Bancroft. She was stretched out on a cushion upon which she must have fallen. For an instant, as he gazed at her features as pale as marble, and her closed eyes, a dreadful thought flashed across Roy's mind. What if she were dead?

But to his great relief he speedily ascertained that the girl was breathing. An ugly bruise on her forehead may have accounted for her continued swoon although she had fainted with terror the instant the train appeared beneath them on the crossing.

The car, its hood crumpled up as if it had been made of paper instead of metal, stood at the foot of a tree not far off.

"No wonder we were thrown out," thought Roy, as he gazed at the wreck and considered the speed at which they had encountered the obstruction. "The wonder is we escaped with our lives."

After a brief and ineffectual attempt to arouse the girl the boy looked about him for some means of assistance. The cowardly train crew had not stopped when they saw the accident. Visions of damage suits and summary discharges may have drifted through their minds, for extra freights were supposed to send flagmen to the crossing to warn all traffic of the train's approach.

Suddenly Roy recollected the two men he had seen spring from behind the hedge as the runaway auto approached the gap. What had become of them? Apparently they had taken to their heels also, for not a sign was to be seen of them.

"Odd," thought the boy to himself; "one would think the first instinct of a human being at seeing an accident like this would be to stay and help. But, hold on, maybe they've gone for a doctor. A retired physician, Dr. Mays, lives not far from here. In the meantime if I could only get some cold water."

Suddenly he spied a small brook at the foot of the hill. Ill and dazed as he felt Roy sprinted toward it, and wetting his handkerchief hastened back to Jess. Kneeling by her side he bathed her forehead. He was rewarded in a few moments by beholding her eyelids flutter and open. In a few seconds more she was fully conscious, but weak and shaken. Roy collected the scattered cushions from the wreck, and placing them like a mattress laid the girl upon them.

She thanked him with a wan smile and then lay still once more. Roy wisely did not speak. He judged that perfect quiet was what she wanted at that moment.

While he sat by her side meditating what to do a sudden noise caused him to look upward.

It was a noise like the drone of a giant bumble bee. It came from directly above his head.

"The Golden Butterfly!" shouted Roy, springing to his feet.

Above him, at an elevation of some thousand feet, the yellow wings of the Prescott aeroplane were outlined against the blue, like the form of one of her namesakes.

Roy shouted and waved frantically. Presently he was rewarded by the flutter of a handkerchief from the chassis of the 'plane. At the same instant it was swung about, and revolving in graceful circles began to spiral down to the earth.

"Hooray! It's Peggy and Jimsy!" cried Roy. "I recollect now Jess told me that Jimsy was to have a lesson to-day."

Ten minutes later the aeroplane lighted in the field not a hundred yards from the wreck. As it reached the ground Peggy started the engine at reduced speed. The aerial marvel began to scoot across the field toward Roy as obediently as if it had been an automobile under perfect control.

Agitated as he was Roy could not help feeling enthusiastic as the huge, glittering, flying thing came closer, its engine roaring and its propeller whirring angrily, and yet, the dainty girl in the motor bonnet who was driving it had it under perfect control every second. Throwing back a lever and cutting off the spark and the gasolene, Peggy brought the aeroplane to a stop with a jerk.

Jimsy, with alarmed questions on his lips, sprang out, while Roy helped his sister to alight.

"Good gracious, whatever has happened?" gasped the girl, as she stood on the ground and viewed the still form of her chum Jess, over which Jimsy was bending in genuine alarm.

"It's all right, sis," Roy assured her, "Jess is not badly hurt. See— she is looking up at you."

Peggy sped lightly over the turf to her chum's side.

"Oh, Peggy, dear, I'm so glad you've come. It was dreadful. But Roy was so brave. I'm sure I owe my life to him, for the last thing I recollect we were heading direct for the train."

She would have said more, but Peggy held up an admonitory finger. Turning to Roy she sought an explanation of all that occurred.

It was soon told, and then the question of summoning a physician came up.

In the midst of the discussion Peggy gave a glad little cry.

"The aeroplane! I can fly over to Doctor Mays' house. There's a dandy big pasture in the rear in which to alight."

"By George, that's so," agreed Roy, "and I guess, although it sounds a bit startling, it's the only thing to do. We can't run the car and nobody will be along here for hours perhaps. This road isn't travelled much."

But Peggy, with that quick decision which was characteristic of her, was already half way to the aeroplane. A moment more and she was in the chassis, and slipping into the driver's seat began adjusting the motor.

"I'll leave you to look after Jess," said Roy to Jimsy, "while I go along with Peggy. I'm not sure that she is as expert in managing an aeroplane as she thinks she is."

"Well, she brought me over here at a great rate, anyhow," put in Jimsy, loyally.

"And in the nick of time, too," said Roy, warmly pressing the other's hand.

"Oh, do be back as quickly as possible, my foot hurts dreadfully," moaned poor Jess, "and my head feels as if a thousand dwarfs were hammering away inside it."

"We'll be back before you expect us," Roy said, cheerily. Jimsy shouted something, but his words were drowned in the roar of the motor as Roy clambered into the Golden Butterfly and Peggy started the engine.

The aeroplane dashed forward over the smooth turf and then seemed to take the air as lightly and easily as a bit of gossamer. Straight up it soared, high above the tree tops, and was speedily reduced to a fast diminishing speck in the northwest in which direction lay Doctor Mays' home. Looking downward from the speeding flyer the boy and girl aviators could see, spread out below them like a checkerboard, the fertile Long Island landscape.

Through it ran the railroad, looking like a glittering ribbon of steel. Off to the north the sea sparkled, a few white sails dotting its surface.

The Black Rock lighthouse, painted in bands of red and white, formed a conspicuous object.

All at once, on the road beneath them, Roy spied a solitary motor-cyclist whom, even at the height to which they had now risen, he recognized as Fanning Harding. He called his sister's attention to the rider.

"He must have passed right by where the accident happened," he remarked; "that road has no outlet for some distance. Funny that he didn't come to help us."

"You must remember that the banks and hedge hid the place from the road," Peggy reminded him. "Even Fanning Harding wouldn't have willfully passed by you when you were in such straits."

"I don't think so, either," agreed Roy, "and come to think of it, bending over his handlebars as he is, he would not be likely to have noticed the gap we ploughed through."

"Look," cried Peggy suddenly, "he's stopping."

The girl was right. The motor-cycling boy, whose pace had hitherto been as fast as that of the aeroplane, could now be seen to slacken his machine and finally stop it. Leaning it against a fence he clambered into an adjoining field, and with every evidence of extreme caution he crept toward a patch of woods at no great distance.

"What can he be doing?" exclaimed Peggy.

As she spoke they saw the boy below them take something from his hip pocket.

"A pistol!" cried Roy.

The next instant Fanning Harding had vanished into the patch of woods without having noticed the aerial observers, or, at least, so it appeared.

CHAPTER VI.
A ROADSIDE MYSTERY.

"Now, what could he be up to?" Roy wondered as they sped on.

"Give it up," laughed Peggy, "unless he was going rabbit shooting."

"Rabbit shooting with a pistol—and in June—oh, Peggy, I thought you were more of a sport than that."

"Well, can you suggest any solution?"

"Frankly—no. But I've been forgetting something which the sight of Fanning Harding reminded me of," and Roy at once plunged into an account of his interview with the banker and his son.

To his great relief Peggy agreed with him that on no account must the aeroplane be turned over to the Hardings, but her mind was sadly troubled, nevertheless, by what her brother told her concerning Simon Harding's attitude.

"It looks as if he was bent on hounding us," she sighed.

"It surely does," agreed Roy, "but look, sis—there's Doctor Mays' house off there. You'll have to make a landing in that field back of the barn."

Peggy nodded and deftly touched a lever or two. The aeroplane began to descend.

"Want me to take the helm?" inquired Roy.

If Peggy had dared to turn her head she would have flashed an indignant glance at her brother. As it was she had to content herself with a very haughty, "No, indeed."

Roy laughed.

"You surely are the original Girl Aviator," he exclaimed.

"Huh!" cried Peggy, "by no means the original one, my dear. There are lots of them in Europe and there soon will be in this country, too."

"I hope so," responded Roy, "riding with a pretty girl in an aeroplane just suits me."

But Peggy did not reply, and for a good reason. They were now just above the pasture lot in which she meant to descend, and below them, as they dropped, an amusing scene was transpiring.

The Doctor's horse, old Dobbin, was dashing madly around in circles, faster than he had gone in twenty years of solid respectability; the two cows, and an old mother pig with her family, joined him as the strange whirring thing from the sky dropped lowering above them. As for the chickens, they flew wildly in every direction, clucking as if they had gone mad.

In the midst of the turmoil a rear door opened and a kindly-faced old man with white whiskers and a pair of big spectacles perched on his nose, emerged, to see what could be causing all the disturbance. He fairly dropped the big book he was holding, in his astonishment as he beheld a glistening object, like a huge yellow and spangled bird, dropping in his very back yard, so to speak. But the next instant he recovered himself.

"Bless my soul," exclaimed Dr. Mays, for it was the retired physician himself, "I thought for a moment that the fabled days of the gigantic Roc, with which Sinbad the sailor had his adventures, had returned.

"It must be those Prescott children. Ah!" he exclaimed, as the aeroplane alighted and came to a standstill, "it is! Dear me, what a century we are living in! Boys and girls flying about like—like—my chickens!"

He "clucked" reassuringly to the terrified birds as he hastened toward the now stationary machine. Roy and his sister came forward to greet the venerable old doctor as he approached.

Roy hastily explained their errand, being interrupted constantly by the physician's exclamations of astonishment.

"Go back with you? Of course, I will, my children. Will one of you help me catch old Dobbin and harness him? My man Jake is in town to-day."

"Oh, doctor," cried Peggy, entreatingly, "can't we persuade you to go back with us in the Golden Butterfly?"

"To fly! Good heavens!"

The aged physician threw up his hands at the idea.

"It is perfectly safe, sir," put in Roy. "Safer than old Dobbin in his present frame of mind, I should imagine."

They all had to laugh as they looked at the hitherto staid and sober equine careening about the pasture with his tail held high, and from time to time emitting shrill whinnies of terror at the sight of the strange thing which had landed in his domain.

"I don't know, I really don't," hesitated Dr. Mays. "The very idea of an old man like me riding in an aeroplane. It's—it's—"

"Just splendid," laughed Peggy, merrily, "and, doctor, I've often heard you say to father that it was a physician's duty to keep pace with modern invention."

"Quite right! Quite right! I often told your poor father so," cried Dr. Mays. "Well, my dear, it may be revolutionary and unbecoming to a man of my years, but I actually believe I will brave a new element in that flying machine of yours. More especially as we can reach my young patient much quicker in that way."

While Dr. Mays, who was a widower and childless, went to hunt up an old cap, as headgear for his novel journey, Roy obtained permission to use the doctor's telephone. He called up Jess's home and related briefly to Mrs. Bancroft what had occurred, and asked that an automobile be sent to the scene of the accident.

Mrs. Bancroft, who at first had been seriously alarmed, was reassured by Roy's quiet manner of breaking the news to her, and promised to come over herself at once. By this time Doctor Mays was ready, and the young people noted, not without amusement, that under his assumed air of confidence the benevolent old gentleman was not a little worried at the idea of braving what was to him a new element.

The Golden Butterfly was equipped with a small extension seat at the stern of her chassis, and into this Roy dropped after it had been pulled out. Dr. Mays was seated in the centre, as being the heaviest of the party, while Peggy resumed her place at the steering and driving apparatus.

"All ready behind?" she called out, laughingly, as they settled down.

"All right here, my dear," responded the doctor with an inward conviction that all was wrong.

"Go ahead, sis," cried Roy. "Hold tight, doctor, to those straps on the side."

With a roar and a whirring thunder of its exhausts the motor was started up. Dr. Mays paled, but, as Roy afterward expressed it, "he was dead game." Forward shot the aeroplane across the hitherto peaceful pasture lot which was now turned into a crazy circus of terrified animals.

"Wh-wh-when are we going up?"

The doctor asked the question rather jerkily as the aeroplane sped over the uneven ground, jolting, and jouncing tremendously despite its chilled-steel spiral springs.

"In a moment," explained Roy; "the extra weight makes her slower in rising than usual."

"Look out, child!" yelled the doctor, suddenly, "you'll crash into the fence."

He half rose, but Roy pulled him back.

"It's all right, doctor," he said reassuringly.

But to the physician it seemed far otherwise. The fence he had alluded to, a tall, five-barred, white-washed affair, loomed right up in front of them. It seemed as if the aeroplane, scudding over the ground like a scared jackrabbit, must crash into it.

But no such thing happened.

As the 'plane neared the obstruction something seemed to impel it upward. Peggy pulled a lever and twisted a valve, and the motor, beating like a fevered pulse, answered with an angry roar.

The Golden Butterfly rose gracefully, just grazing the fence top, like a jumping horse. But, unlike the latter, it did not come down upon the other side. Instead, it soared upward in a steady gradient.

The doctor, his first alarm over, gazed about him with wonder, and perhaps a bit of awe. Many times had he and his dead friend, Mr. Prescott, talked over aerial possibilities, and he had always listened with interest to what the inventor had to say. But that he should actually be riding in such a marvellous craft seemed like a dream to this venerable man of science.

After his first feeling of alarm had worn off the physician found that riding in an aeroplane after the preliminary run with its bumps and jouncings is over, is very like drifting gently over the fleeciest of clouds in a gossamer car, if such a thing can be imagined. In other words, the Golden Butterfly seemed not to be moving fast, but to be floating in the crystal clear atmosphere. But a glance over the edge of the high-sided chassis soon showed the physician that she was tearing along at a great rate at a height of about five hundred feet. Fields, woods, streams and small farmhouses swam by beneath their keel.

"Well, doctor, how do you like it?" Roy ventured, after a few moments.

"Like it!" repeated the physician; "my lad, it's—it's—it's bully!"

And thus did his dignity fall like a mantle from Doctor Mays after a few moments in Peggy Prescott's, the girl aviator's, Golden Butterfly.

A few moments later they came in sight of the field in which they had left poor Jess lying by the side of the wrecked automobile.

Hardly had they alighted before Jimsy, a rather worried look on his face, was at the side of the aeroplane.

"Say, Roy," he exclaimed, "you didn't happen to put that jewel case in your pocket for safe keeping after the accident, did you?"

"Why, no. Jess had it and slipped it under the seat while she was driving," cried Roy. "Why?"

"Because it's gone!" exclaimed Jimsy, somewhat blankly.

"Gone! Impossible!" protested Roy.

"But it is. I've searched the field thoroughly in the vicinity of the car, and I can't find a single trace of it."

"It couldn't have been stolen."

It was Peggy who spoke.

Roy thought a moment. All at once the recollection of Fanning Harding's queer actions when they had seen him on the road below them flashed into his mind. The road, as he had observed, led past the scene of the accident.

Would it have been possible for Fanning to enter the field while they lay unconscious there? After an instant's figuring Roy had to dismiss the idea. Had such been the case, the son of the banker would have been much further off when they observed him from the aeroplane than he had been. The speed he was making would have carried him far from the wrecked auto had he been near it at the time the accident occurred.

What, then, could have become of the jewel case?

"It must be here," exclaimed Roy, positively; "nobody could have taken it."

While Dr. Mays bent over Jess and examined her injured ankle the others searched the field in every reasonable direction. But not a trace of the jewel case could they find.

All at once, the noise of a horse's hoofs coming at a rapid trot was heard from the road. Roy, thinking it might be some one of whom he might make inquiries, hastened to the hedge and peered over. He saw, coming toward him, a disreputable-looking old ramshackle rig, driven by a red-haired man of big frame who was slouchily dressed. His chin had once been shaven, but now the hair stood out on it like bristles on an old tooth brush. By the side of this individual was seated none other than the immaculate Fanning Harding, in his motor-cycling clothes.

"Why, that's Gid Gibbons, the most disreputable character about here," exclaimed Roy, in amazement. "What can Fan Harding be doing with him?"

He now noted, to his further astonishment and perplexity, that there was a third person in the rig—Gid Gibbon's daughter, a pretty girl in a coarse way, and given to loud dressing. She had plenty of black hair and a pair of dark eyes that might have been beautiful if they had not had a certain hard, defiant look in them.

As they drew near Fan Harding turned and seemed to whisper something to the girl, whose name was Hester, at which they both laughed heartily.

CHAPTER VII.
PEGGY IS PUZZLED.

"Hello, Gid," hailed Roy, thinking that perhaps the ne'er-do-well, who conducted a small blacksmith shop some distance off, might be able to throw some light on the mystery.

"Hello, yourself," was the response in a harsh, gutteral voice as Gid drew in his reins and the conveyance came to a stop. Roy raised his hat to Hester Gibbons and nodded coldly to Fan Harding.

"Good gracious, what's been happening?" shrilled out the girl.

"An accident," said Roy, and went on rapidly to explain what had occurred.

"And the worst of it is," the boy went on, "that besides the accident Miss Bancroft has suffered a serious loss. A wallet containing valuable jewelry has vanished entirely." Roy watched Fan Harding closely as he spoke and thought that he saw him change color. It might have likewise been fancy, but he could have sworn that the girl, too, looked confused. Gid puckered up his lips and emitted a whistle.

"Lost a wallet with jewelry in it, eh?" he repeated.

"Have you looked everywhere for it?" asked Fan Harding, with an appearance of great solicitude.

"Everywhere we can think of," rejoined Roy. He turned to Jimsy, who had just joined him. Jimsy looked despondent and worried. A glance at his countenance convinced Roy that the jewel case was still missing.

"I'll get out and help you look for it myself," said Fan Harding suddenly. "It's awfully queer. Miss Bancroft remarked when she left the bank that she would take particular care of the jewels."

"I wonder if any one passed on this road while we were unconscious?" queried Roy, looking narrowly at Fan.

To his surprise, the other answered with a great show of frankness.

"It's very odd," he exclaimed, "but I myself must have gone by this place not more than a few moments after the smash-up. I was on my way to Gid Gibbons's blacksmith shop to get a part of my motorcycle fixed up. I guess if I hadn't been bending over my brakes as I rode down hill I'd have seen the place myself."

"Guess so," struck in Gid, with a grin; "no one never accused you of being blind."

"My motor-cycle was in worse repair than I thought," went on Fan, "and so I left it at Gid's place and accepted his offer to ride into town with him."

This all sounded plausible enough. Yet Roy noted that Fan had not mentioned his little excursion into the wood with the pistol. What was he trying to conceal? What had been his mission there?

While these thoughts flashed through Roy's mind Gid and his daughter had followed Fan's example and now joined the searchers. By this time, Jess, under the doctor's ministrations, was able to sit up. Her face was pale as marble, partly from suffering, for her ankle still gave her considerable pain, and partly from agitation at the loss of the jewels.

There was a sudden puffing of an auto, and presently Mrs. Bancroft herself, in a smaller car than the wrecked one, was driven into the group by one of the employees of her husband's estate. As gently as possible, after first explanations had been made, Jess broke the news to her. Mrs. Bancroft, a tall, stately woman, went white as she heard.

"One of those jewels, a ruby, was an heirloom that has been in the family for years," she exclaimed. "I would not have lost it for all the others. Has every place been searched thoroughly?"

"Everywhere, mamma," responded Jess.

"Bin over ther ground with a fine tooth comb, mum," said the uncouth Gid.

Mrs. Bancroft raised her lorgnette and regarded the unabashed Gid with a look tinged with some disgust. But Gid merely showed his yellow fangs, in what he intended to be a pleasant smile, in reply, and lifted his hat with clumsy gallantry.

"What was the last you saw of the jewels?" asked Mrs. Bancroft of her daughter, after Jess had been tenderly carried to the other auto and made comfortable.

"It was just before we started down the hill," was the reply. "I felt to see if it was safe under the seat just before the car got away from me."

"Then they were there just before the accident, of course," put in Mrs. Bancroft. "And now they are missing in this mysterious way."

"Well, they couldn't have walked off," said Fan; "somebody may have taken them while you were unconscious. Unless—"

He stopped and glanced at Roy, who felt his face flushing angrily. There had been a queer intonation in Fan Harding's tones.

"Unless what?" put in Jess, looking at Fan Harding directly in the eyes. His dropped under the scrutiny of the straightforward girl.

"I suppose you mean unless I took them," struck in Roy, angrily. There was a hard note of defiance in his tones which sounded strange there.

Fan Harding glanced at him quickly and then said in a low voice:

"Well, it does look odd, you know, and—"

"Don't dare to say another word like that!"

Peggy, her soft eyes blazing, stepped forward before Mrs. Bancroft could stop her. Gid Gibbon's daughter watched the angry girl with a contemptuous smile. But Fan Harding went white and shrank back.

"I—I didn't mean anything," he stammered.

"Children! Children!" exclaimed Mrs. Bancroft, "no more of this. It seems that there is a mystery here, and perhaps some day it will be solved. But in the meantime I wish no suspicion, or doubt even, cast on any one."

If they had been watching Fan Harding they would have seen his face brighten up at this. Muttering something in an undertone to Gid, he slunk off, accompanied by his disreputable blacksmith companion and the latter's daughter, Hester, as she went, flung back a glance of contempt at the others, of which they took not the slightest notice.

Dr. Mays elected to return home by means of Mrs. Bancroft's auto. He declared, laughingly, that he had had quite enough excitement that morning for a man of his years. A few moments after the departure of Fan and his strange companions therefore, Mrs. Bancroft's auto, towing the injured car by means of a rope brought along for that purpose, set out on its return journey. Jimsy rode beside his sister, who made a brave effort to bid a cheery good-bye to the young aviators.

But, somehow, all of them felt that a constraint had been suddenly born among them, arising out of the mystery of the missing jewels. The next day posters, announcing a reward for the recovery of the jewels, were hurriedly struck off at Sandy Bay printing office, and distributed throughout the town and the surrounding country. In due course the Prescott household, of course, received one, and the perusal of it did not add to their cheerfulness.

The bills gave a description of the accident and the circumstances, and Roy could not but feel that any logical person reading the things would come to the conclusion that Roy Prescott probably knew more about the facts of the case, at least, than any one else.

In addition to the disconcerting bills the regular police officials of Sandy Bay visited the Prescott home and interrogated Roy, to Peggy's huge indignation. But worse was to come; private detectives also came and questioned and cross-questioned him at great length. Roy could not but feel with all this that he was an object of suspicion, but he bravely went about as before and tried to hide his inner thoughts as closely as possible.

Jess soon recovered and was up and about once more. The four young folks interchanged visits and motored and "aeroed" together as freely as before, but they somehow all felt that the air was charged with some influence that made things quite different to what they had been before the accident and the subsequent mysterious vanishing of the jewels.

Peggy privately made up her mind, with a truly feminine intuition, that Fanning Harding had something to do with the affair. Recalling his strange visit to the wood, she even visited the place by herself one day to see if she could light upon any clew that might serve to clear things up. But, as might have been expected, she found nothing.

Her trip over had been made in the Golden Butterfly. Disappointed at her lack of success, for she had almost allowed herself to believe that she would, in some queer fashion, happen upon a clew, the girl was preparing to return, when something happened.

A rod, connecting a warping lever with the right wing of the monoplane, snapped with a sharp crack.

"Oh, dear!" exclaimed Peggy to herself, "what shall I do?"

She looked about her as if seeking for information from her surroundings. All at once she became aware that two men had emerged from the wood behind her and were watching her closely.

Plucky as the girl was, she felt her heart beat a little quicker as she gazed. There was something so very piercing in their scrutiny.

Suddenly one of them stepped forward, and Peggy saw, to her astonishment, that she knew him. More astonishing still, the man was trembling and whitefaced as if in alarm at something.

It was Morgan, the butler at Mrs. Bancroft's.

"Why, Morgan, whatever are you doing here?" exclaimed Peggy as she breathed more freely.

The man hesitated. His companion, whom Peggy could now see was an employe about the Bancroft stables, came to his rescue.

"Why, miss, we've been doin' a bit of trapping in the woods there."

"Yes, miss, that's hit," struck in Morgan, a stout, puffy-faced Englishman with "side burns."

"A bit o' poaching, as you might say, miss. I 'opes you won't tell on hus."

"Good gracious, no," laughed Peggy, immensely relieved to find that the two men were not strangers. "I thought you looked scared when you saw me, Morgan."

"Yes, miss. You see, I haint used in hold England ter see young ledies a flyin' round like bloomin'—bloomin' pertater bugs, hif you'll pardon the comparison, miss. But 'as yer 'ad han h'accident?"

"I have," rejoined Peggy, restraining an impulse to say "I 'ave." "It's not much. If there was a blacksmith shop round here I could get it fixed in a jiffy. It's just this rod that's snapped."

"Why, miss," puffed Morgan, "Gid Gibbon's place isn't more than a few paces, as you might say, from 'ere. Why don't you take that rod there? Hi'll h'escort yer."

"Why, that's so," agreed Peggy, "how stupid of me not to have thought of it. Gid can fix it in a few minutes."

Selecting a small wrench from the tool box Peggy deftly unbolted the broken rod, and then, with Morgan and his companion as guides, she set off across the fields for Gid's shop, which she now recalled was a short distance up the road, but hidden from the spot where the Butterfly had dropped by a patch of woods.

"By the way, Morgan," the girl asked, suddenly, "has anything more been heard of the missing jewels?"

To Peggy's astonishment the man started and stammered.

"Yes, miss—that is—no, miss. I means, miss, that there ain't been no news, miss, hof hany kind, miss."

Peggy nodded without appearing to note the man's confusion.

"It's a queer affair, miss," put in Morgan's companion, whose name was Giles.

"It is, indeed," rejoined Peggy. "I do wish it could all be cleared up."

"Same 'ere, miss, hi'm sure," struck in Morgan, mopping his puffy face. He seemed to have, in great part, recovered his composure.

"Well, there is the blacksmith shop," said the other man presently, as they emerged from the fields upon the road through a sliding gate. He pointed to a long, low, ramshackle structure at the cross-roads. Beside it stood a fairly neat cottage and beyond this again a brand new shed, from which proceeded a great sound of hammering.

As Morgan and Giles left her, to make a shortcut home across lots, Peggy set off at a brisk pace, holding the broken rod in her hands. She almost dropped the bits of metal an instant later in a great surprise that she encountered.

The door of the brand new building opened and out stepped Fanning Harding, in overalls and jumper. Suddenly he became aware of Peggy's advancing figure and halted, staring at her.

CHAPTER VIII.
HESTER'S RUBY.

The door of the shed had been opened wide, but Fanning closed it swiftly as if in great anxiety to conceal what was within. Then it was that Peggy first became aware of something she had not noticed before. Above the portal was a signboard upon which was painted in staring red letters:

"Office and Works of the Fanning Harding Aeroplane Co."

Hardly had Peggy digested this astonishing sign before Fanning, his look of startled surprise replaced by a smile, advanced, cap in hand, to meet her.

"Why, what ever brings you here?" he asked, with the air of easy familiarity which Peggy disliked so much. "I guess that that sign gave you a kind of a start, eh?"

"It certainly did," agreed Peggy, "and it gives me even more of a start to see you working, Fanning."

"Huh," grunted the youth, beneath whose blue overalls were visible a pair of gaudy socks of the kind he affected, "I guess you think that I can't make good as well as any one else when I try. Roy wouldn't go into a deal with me on that aeroplane of his, so I just got busy and started a concern of my own."

"Do you mean you are actually building an aeroplane?"

"Yes. Got orders for several of them," rejoined the swaggering youth. "So far I've only had Gid to help me, but I guess I'll have to enlarge the plant pretty soon. You see that Roy would have been wiser to sell me that 'plane of his at the start-off. As things are now, the Harding Aeroplane Company is going to discount anything in its line."

"Well, I am glad of that," said Peggy, briskly, and with some trace of asperity. Fanning's conceited, confident air jarred upon her sadly.

"But I came over here to find Mr. Gibbons. I want him to repair this rod for me."

"Why, that's off an aeroplane!" exclaimed Fanning, eagerly; "you must have come to earth in the Golden Butterfly quite close to here."

"Why, yes. In that field yonder," rejoined Peggy, some instinct telling her not to disclose the true object of her visit there; "my motor went wrong and I had to descend."

"What field did you come down in? That one by the clump of woods round the bend in the road?" asked Fanning, with just a trace of anxiety in his tone.

"Yes. It was lucky I was so close. Morgan and Giles—"

"What, Morgan and Giles were there?"

Fanning seemed tremendously excited all of a sudden.

"Why, yes. What of it?"

But Fanning had pulled himself together.

"Oh, nothing," he said, in a matter-of-fact tone. "I only thought they were a long way from home, that's all. But here comes Gid now. Hey, Gid! Miss Prescott wants a rod welded. Can you do it for her right away?"

"Sure," responded the ill-favored blacksmith, shuffling up. His chin was more bristly than ever, and his shifty blue eyes blinked like a rat's beady orbs as he took the bits of metal.

"A flaw," he declared, examining them; "wonder it didn't break sooner. Come on to the forge, miss, and I'll fix it for you in a brace-of-shakes."

Off he shuffled toward the ramshackle forge, Peggy following. Behind her came Fanning. As they passed the cottage Hester Gibbons came flying down the path, but stopped at a sign from Fanning. The youth dropped further behind, and as Peggy followed Gid into the forge and the bellows began roaring, they began to talk in low tones.

"Do you think she can suspect anything?" asked Hester at one point.

"Not a thing," was the confident response. "That pale-faced old gopher, Morgan, was in the wood this afternoon, though. She told me that. The existence of the Harding Aeroplane Company has become known rather before I wanted it to, also. However, they may as well know now as any other time that they aren't the only fliers in the air. I guess the Harding aeroplane will beat anything in its line ever seen."

"I guess it will," laughed Hester, and then, for some unknown reason, they both burst into fits of immoderate laughter. Evidently something connected with Fanning's new enterprise was deemed highly amusing by both of them.

Peggy left without seeing Hester, although from behind a blind in the cottage, the girl watched her closely enough. Gid, whatever his other shortcomings might have been, was a good blacksmith, and the rod was well repaired. Peggy soon had it adjusted, and was about to clamber into the chassis and start home when a shout from the road made her look up. An automobile stood there, and in it were Jess and Jimsy. They hailed her excitedly, and Peggy hastily threw out the switch which she had just adjusted and hastened across the field to them.

She soon saw that Jess was waving a leather pocket case above her head and that her face was flushed and excited.

"My dear Jess, whatever has happened?" she cried, as she came up to the side of the auto.

"Happened!" echoed Jess. "Why, my dear, the most extraordinary, inexplicable thing you ever heard of."

"In other words, 'we are up in the air,'" quoth the slangy Jimsy, "even if we don't own an aeroplane."

"You see this case," cried Jess, extending the leather wallet for Peggy's inspection. "Well, that's the case that held mamma's jewels. It was returned most strangely to us this afternoon. We found it on the porch after lunch.

"Oh, Jess! the jewels were in it. I'm so glad."

"No, girlie, it was empty."

"Empty!" echoed Peggy, "and nobody knows how it came there?"

"No, we must have been at lunch at the time. None of the servants know anything about the matter, either. It's a real, dark and deep mystery."

"It's all of that, my dear Watson," proclaimed Jimsy, folding his arms and scowling in imitation of a famous detective of fiction. "Why on earth should the thief want to return the wallet? You'd think he'd dodge such a risk of being arrested."

But Peggy had been looking at the wallet which had so amazingly reappeared.

"Why, Jess," she cried, "it's all mud-stained. It looks as if it had been buried somewhere."

"It certainly does," agreed Jimsy, "but even that doesn't give us any more to go on than the theory that the jewels have been buried some place."

"And been dug up again," put in Peggy, quickly.

After some more conversation the group was about to break up, when Jess exclaimed suddenly:

"Oh, by the way, did you hear about Jeff Stokes? No, I see you haven't. Well, he's been appointed wireless operator at Rocky Point."

"Oh, I'm so glad," cried Peggy, impulsively; "that's been his ambition for a long time."

Rocky Point was a projecting neck of land about two miles east of Sandy Bay. It was quite an important signalling station for ships passing up and down the Sound. The position which Jeff Stokes had secured was a lucrative one in a way, and, at any rate, was in direct line of promotion.

The two Bancrofts waited to watch Peggy take the air in her now staunch aeroplane. It was not until she had vanished with a whirr and a whiz that Jimsy thought of starting his own car.

"Gracious," cried Jess, as they sped along, "how I wish that the mystery of those jewels could be cleared up."

As she spoke they were passing by the cottage occupied by Gid Gibbons.

"Oh, look, there's that horrid Fanning Harding and Gid Gibbons's daughter at the gate," cried Jess.

At the same instant as she uttered the exclamation, Hester Gibbons looked up in time to see Jess's gaze concentrated upon her. She whisked about, her skirts swinging as she did so. But she did not turn quickly enough for Jess's sharp eyes not to see that she snatched at something she had been wearing at her throat.

The millionaire's daughter was almost certain that the object Hester snatched at in such a hurry was a ruby brooch, or at least an imitation of one. She had distinctly caught a ruddy flash as Hester's hand moved to her throat.

Jimsy, too, had noticed it, it seemed, for he suddenly observed:

"Seems queer for Hester to be wearing jewelry. Her father must be making money fast nowadays."

"Yes," said Jess, but her voice was distant and preoccupied. She was certain that her eyes had not deceived her. It had been a ruby that Hester Gibbons had pulled off and hastened to conceal. Obeying an impulse, she turned and gazed back over the top of the tonneau.

Through the dust cloud behind the car she could see that Hester and Fanning Harding were once more in deep conversation at the gate. She wondered what they could find so engrossing to talk about, and also speculated on several other things. She, however, avoided mentioning her suddenly aroused suspicions to Jimsy. He was so hasty. Inwardly she made a resolve to seek out Peggy the first thing the next day and compare notes with her. She could not help feeling that matters were assuming a very complicated aspect.

CHAPTER IX.
A RACE AGAINST TIME.

One evening, a week later, Peggy and her brother were tightening up some braces on the Golden Butterfly after an afternoon's flight along the coast, when the sharp "honk! honk!" of an automobile from the road attracted their attention. Running to the door, Peggy saw Jimsy and his sister in the "Gee Whizz," as their red auto had been christened.

But that there was something the matter with the Gee Whizz was evident. The motor, ungeared, was coughing and gasping in a painful manner. Jimsy shouted as he saw the two young Prescotts.

"Say, you aviators, come here and see what you can do to doctor a poor creeping earthworm of an auto."

Laughing at his tone and words, Peggy and her brother hastened down the path and through the gate.

"Something's wrong with the transmission," explained Jimsy.

"What's the trouble?" asked Roy.

"What a question, you goose?" cried Jess; "if we knew we'd have fixed it long ago."

"It's doubly annoying," said Jimsy, in an impatient voice, "because we got a wire from father to-night, saying that he would take us on a trip to Washington with him if we arrived in New York by eight-thirty."

"Oh, you poor dears," exclaimed Peggy, "and if you don't get there at that time?"

"We can't go, that's all," said Jess, tragically clasping her gloved hands.

"Bother the luck," muttered Jimsy, with masculine grumpiness. "Found out what's the trouble, Roy?"

"Yes," was the response; "one of your gears is stripped. I'm afraid that there'll be no Washington trip for you folksies."

The tears rose in Jess's fine eyes. Jimsy looked cross, and an abrupt silence fell.

It was Peggy who broke it with a suggestion.

"There's a train leaves Central Riverview junction at six, isn't there?"

"I believe so," rejoined Jess, in a doleful voice; "we took it one night, I remember, when we missed the through cars from Sandy Bay."

"It's five now," nodded Peggy, examining the dial of a tiny watch, one of the last presents her father had given her.

"Fat chance of getting this old hurdy-gurdy fixed up in time to make it," grumbled Jimsy.

"You don't have to," cried Peggy, with a note of triumph.

"Don't have to!"

It was Jess who echoed the remark.

"No, indeed. Our aerial express will start for the junction in a few minutes, and—"

But the rest was drowned in an enthusiastic shout. Jess threw her arms about her chum and fairly hugged her.

"You darling. We can make it?"

"We must," was the business-like rejoinder. "Roy, you get the Butterfly out and fill the lubricator tank. We've got enough gasolene."

Roy and Jimsy, arm in arm, hastened off to the shed. The two girls followed more leisurely. It was not long before everything was in readiness, but fast as they worked it was nearly half an hour before preparations were all complete.

Then they climbed in and Peggy started the engine. But the next instant she shut it off again.

"The second cylinder is missing fire," she pronounced.

Roy bent over the refractory part of the motor and soon had it adjusted. Then the motor settled down to a steady tune, the regular humming throb that delights the heart of the aviator.

"All ready?" inquired Peggy, adjusting her hood and goggles and turning about.

"Right Oh!" hailed Jimsy.

"Now, boys and girls, prepare for a long run," warned Peggy; "with this load it will take a long time to rise."

The aeroplane was speeded up and soon traversed the slope leading from the back of the shed to the summit of the little hill at the rear of the Prescott place. As it topped the rise Peggy turned on full power. The Golden Butterfly dashed forward and then, after what seemed a long interval, began to rise. Up it soared, its motor laboring bravely under its heavy burden. In the dusk blue flames could be seen occasionally spurting from the exhausts. It would have been a weird, perhaps a terrifying sight to any one unused to it—the flight of this roaring, flaming, sky monster, through the evening gloom.

"We've got half an hour to make the twenty miles," shouted Roy, from his seat beside his sister. Peggy set her little white even teeth and nodded.

"I'm going to make for the tracks and follow them. That's the quickest way," she said.

It seemed only a few seconds later that the red and green lights of a semaphore signal flashed up below them.

"Bradley's Crossing," announced Roy.

Swinging the aeroplane about, Peggy began flying directly above the tracks.

"No sign of the train yet—we may make it," said Jimsy, pulling out his watch. It showed a quarter to six, and they had fifteen miles to travel, or so Roy estimated the distance.

"Let her out for a mile-a-minute," he exclaimed.

Peggy only nodded. She was far too busy getting all the work she could out of the motor. An extra passenger makes a lot of difference to an aeroplane, and the Butterfly was only built to accommodate three. But she was answering gallantly to the strain.

On she flew above the tracks, every now and then roaring above some astonished crossing keeper or track-walker.

Suddenly, from somewhere behind them, they heard a long, moaning whistle.

"The train!" shouted Jess.

In her excitement she gripped Roy's arm tightly and peered back.

All at once, around a curve, the locomotive came into view—black smoke spouting from its funnel and a column of white steam pouring from its safety valves.

"She'll beat us," cried Jimsy, despairingly, as the thunder of the speeding train grew louder. The setting sun flashed on the varnished sides of the cars.

The engineer thrust his head out of the cab window and gazed upward. His attention had been attracted by the roaring of the motor overhead.

He broke into a yell and waved his hand as he saw the flying aeroplane dashing along above him. The next instant his hand sought the whistle cord.

"Toot! toot! toot!"

The occupants of the aeroplane waved their hands. To their chagrin, however, they saw that, overloaded as the aeroplane was, the train was gaining on them in leaps and bounds. Its windows were black with heads now as passengers, regardless of the danger of encountering some trackside obstacle, leaned out and gazed up at the Golden Butterfly roaring along like some great Thunder Lizard of the dark ages.

"Don't they stop anywhere between here and the junction?" gasped Jimsy.

Roy shook his head.

"It's a through train from Montauk," he said; "they make all the speed they can."

"Two minutes," cried Jess, suddenly; "we won't do it."

But Peggy had suddenly swung off the tracks and was cutting across country. She had seen that the track took a long curve just before it entered the junction. By taking a direct "crow flight" across country she might beat it after all.

And she did. As the train came thundering into the station and stopped with a mighty screaming of brakes and hiss of escaping steam, the aeroplane came to earth in the flat park-like space in front of the depot.

"Tumble out quick!" shouted Roy, "she only stops a jiffy."

Jess and Jimsy lost no time in obeying.

"Good-bye, you darlings!" cried Jess, as she sped after her brother toward the station.

"We'll get our tickets on the train!" shouted Jimsy, as they vanished.

"All ab-o-a-r-d!"

The conductor's voice ran peremptorily out. He had seen the race between the aeroplane and the train, but even that could not disturb a conductor's desire to start on time.

As the wheels began to revolve, Jimsy and Jess swung on to the steps of the rear parlor car. As they did so the passengers broke into an involuntary cheer. The shouts of approval at the up to date manner in which the young folks had "made their train," mingled with the puffing of the locomotive as it sped off.

Among the spectators of the sensational feat had been a broad-shouldered, bronzed man in a big sombrero hat, who sat in the same parlor car which Jimsy and Jess had entered. He looked like a Westerner. As the train gathered headway he suddenly, after an interval of deep thought, struck one big brawny hand upon his knee and exclaimed to himself:

"It's the very thing—the very thing. With a fleet of those I could develop the Jupiter and astonish the mining world."

He rose, with the slowness of a powerful man, and made his way back to where Jimsy and Jess were sitting. Raising his broad-brimmed hat with old-fashioned courtesy, he addressed himself to Jimsy and was soon deep in conversation with him.

CHAPTER X.
THE RIVAL AEROPLANE.

In the meanwhile, the exciting race against time had resulted in overheating the Golden Butterfly's cylinders, and a stop of an hour or more at the junction was necessary. Thus it was quite dark when the young Prescotts were ready to make for home. A small crowd had gathered to see them start, for there was a little community of houses scattered about the junction.

They decided to go the way they had come, namely, to follow the tracks to the crossing and then turn off for home. It was their first experience in night piloting, and when they were ready Peggy switched on the tiny shaded bulb that illuminated the compass. This done, she started the engine, and the Golden Butterfly shot into the air under its reduced load with an almost buoyant sense of freedom.

The crossing was reached in several minutes less than it had taken them to reach the junction on the going trip. Peggy turned off as she marked the glowing lights beneath her, and presently the Golden Butterfly was skimming along above dark woodlands and gloom-enshrouded meadows. There was something awe inspiring about this night flying. Above them the canopy of the stars stretched like a mantle spangled with silver sequins. Below, the earth showed as a black void.

They were flying slowly to avoid overheating the cylinders again. Suddenly a bright glare shot up against the night from below, and a little ahead of them. It died down almost instantly, only to flash up once more.

"Gid Gibbons's forge!" exclaimed Roy. "Let's fly over by there and see what he's doing."

"All right," agreed Peggy; "ever since my visit there I have felt a great interest in Mr. Gibbons. But we'll have to make haste, there's some wind coming before long."

The girl was right. A filmy mist, like a veil, had spread over the stars, dimming their bright lamps, and a wind was beginning to sigh in the trees under them.

But they had not reached Gid Gibbons's place, or rather a location above it, when an astonishing thing happened. From the ground a red light and a green light set at some distance apart began to rise. Up and up they climbed through the night in long, swinging circles. Between them was dimly visible the dark outlines of some fabric.

"An aeroplane!" cried the boy and girl, simultaneously.

"Fan Harding's aeroplane!" cried Peggy, an instant later.

"And—oh, Roy—it can fly!" she added, admiringly.

"No doubt of that," was the rather grudging reply, as the red and green lights soared up and up.

"Keep clear of it, sis, we don't want a collision," warned Roy.

"Oh, I'd like to get close and see it," breathed Peggy. "I never would have credited Fan Harding with being able to do it."

"Nor I," exclaimed Roy, his dislike of Fan Harding giving place to admiration—genuine admiration—of the other's ingenuity.

"Well, he's beaten me out at my own particular specialty," he exclaimed presently, after an interval in which the lights had climbed far above the Golden Butterfly. "That's a better machine than ours, Peg."

"I guess we'll have to admit that," rejoined the girl, with a sigh. "I wonder if he'll enter for the prize?"

"Of course. With a craft like that he'd be foolish if he didn't. Odd that he's trying it out at night, though."

"I suppose he wants to keep secret what it can do and then spring it on an astonished world," rejoined Peggy. "Good gracious!" she broke off hurriedly.

The aeroplane had given a sudden lurch, and at the same instant a sharp puff of wind struck them both in the face. Peggy's hands fairly flashed among her levers, and she averted what might have been a bad predicament.

Involuntarily, at the same instant, Roy had glanced up at the other aeroplane to see how it was faring. To his astonishment the lights did not seem to waver.

"Wow, Peg!" he cried, "that puff didn't even bother Fan Harding's craft. It was uncanny to see her weather it."

"There's something uncanny about it altogether," sniffed Peggy; "it's a regular phantom airship."

"That's just what it is," agreed Roy, "but I'm afraid it is a substantial enough phantom to carry off that $5,000 prize."

Another puff prevented Peggy from replying just then. Once more the Golden Butterfly careened violently, and then, under Peggy's skillful handling, righted herself. But this time the puff was followed by a steady rush of wind.

"Better turn, Peg, before it gets any worse," advised Roy; "we're off our course now."

"I—I tried to," exclaimed Peggy, desperately, "but the wind won't let me. I don't dare to."

"We must," exclaimed Roy, with a serious note in his voice; "if this wind freshens much more we won't be able to turn at all."

He leaned forward and took the wheel from his sister. But the instant he tried to steer the aeroplane round, the wind, rising under one wing tip, careened her to a perilous angle.

"No go," he said; "we've got to keep on going."

"But where can we land?" asked Peggy, a little catch in her voice.

"We'll have to take chances on that," decided Roy. "It would be suicidal to try to buck this wind."

The breeze had now freshened till it was singing an Aeolian song in every wire and brace of the Golden Butterfly. Brother and sister could feel the stout fabric vibrate under the strain of the blast.

The aeroplane was moving swiftly now. But it was the toy of the wind, which grew stronger every minute. The dark landscape beneath fairly flew by under them. Neither of them thought to look back at the red and green lights in the sky behind them.

All at once, Roy, who had leaned over his sister's shoulder and glanced at the compass, gave a sharp cry.

"We've got to turn, sis," he said, in a tense, sharp voice.

"What do you mean, Roy? Are we in any very serious danger?"

The girl's voice shook nervously in response to the anxiety expressed in her brother's tone.

"Danger!" echoed Roy. "Girlie, we are being blown out to sea!"

Blown out to sea! The words held a real poignant terror for Peggy.

"Oh, Roy, we must do something!" she cried, helplessly.

"Yes, but what? We can't, we daren't turn about. The machine would tip like a bucket. No, we must keep on and trust to luck."

Peggy shuddered. Hurtled along in the wind-driven darkness, brother and sister sat in silence, waiting for the first warning that they were approaching the sea.

In the blackness it was impossible to see anything ahead, and the starlight, which, dim as it was, might have helped, had been overcast by a filmy covering of light clouds.

Once or twice as they were hurried helplessly along, the propeller beating desperately against the wind, they saw, far below them, the cheerful lights of some farmhouse. Further off a glare against the sky indicated the lights of Sandy Bay.

How they wished that they were safe and sound at home, as they were blown onward by the wind, going faster and faster every minute.

Roy, his pulses beating hard, and every nerve at tension, had taken the wheel from his sister, even at the risk of careening the aeroplane when they shifted their positions. Every now and then he tried to turn ever so little, but each time a tip at a dangerous angle warned him not to attempt such a thing.

All at once Peggy uttered a shrill cry.

"Oh, Roy! The sea!"

Above the screeching of the wind and the hum of the motor they could now hear another sound, the thunder of the surf on the beach.

Straining his eyes ahead Roy could see now the white gleam of the breakers as they broke in showers of spray on the seashore. A real sense of terror, such as he had never felt before, clutched at his heart as he heard and saw.

But controlling his voice, he turned to Peggy.

"Be brave, little sister," he said; "we'll pull through all right."

Peggy said nothing in response. She dared not trust her voice to speak just at that moment. White faced and with staring, fixed eyes, she sat motionless and silent, as the Golden Butterfly was driven out above the roaring surf and the tossing waves. To her alarmed imagination the sea seemed to be reaching up hungry arms for the two daring young aviators.

Suddenly she was half blinded by a brilliant flash of light which bathed the aeroplane in a flood of radiance. The next instant it was gone, but they could see the great shaft of radiance sweeping around the compass.

"It's the light!" cried Roy. "The Rocky Point light!"

CHAPTER XI.
IN DIREST PERIL.

"Oh, if we could only work round and land on the point," exclaimed Peggy. "There's a fine, smooth field there; in fact, it's all bare ground, without rocks or trees."

"Yes, and Jeff Stokes is wireless operator there, too," rejoined her brother. "Hullo," he exclaimed an instant later, "the wind is shifting a bit. I almost got her head round that time."

"Then there is a chance, Roy!"

"Yes, sis, but don't count too much on it."

Like a skillful jockey handling a restive horse, Roy worked the Golden Butterfly about on the shifting air currents. If once he could turn her nose toward the land he was sure that he would be able to make the ground by driving the aeroplane down on a slanting angle.

Once or twice, while he strove with hand and brain against the elements, he caught his breath with a gasping intake—so near had they come to overturning. But, thanks to the wind eddies of the point, it was possible, after a deal of breathless maneuvering, to get the aeroplane headed for the land.

The instant he found himself in this position Roy threw on all his power and then, "bucking" the wind, like a ship beating up to windward, he rushed down through the night upon the point. As he did so the rays of the slowly revolving light flashed brightly upon the laboring aeroplane. In the radiance it looked like some struggling night bird beating its way against the storm and darkness.

As Peggy had said, the point was clear of rocks or brush, and a landing was made without much difficulty once the aeroplane had been turned. Just as a ship can face the waves with comparative security, so an aeroplane, being driven into the teeth of a gale, is secure so long as she does not "broach to"; in other words, get sidewise to the blast. It was touch and go with the Golden Butterfly for several minutes, though, during that struggle with the elements, and two more thankful young hearts rarely beat than Peggy's and Roy's as they stepped from the machine and made it fast by pointed braces provided for the purpose.

Hardly had she touched the ground before a door in the lower part of the lighthouse opened and the form of Jeff Stokes emerged. He told them that the struggle with the wind had been seen by the light-keeper and himself, and he was warm in his congratulations of the daring young aviators. The light-keeper, a grizzled man named Zeb. Beasley, followed close on Jeff's heels.

"Come right into the house and hev some supper," he said warmly. "It's only rough fare, but you're welcome. My misses will be glad to have you."

Truth to tell, both Peggy and her brother were almost famished and worn out after the tension of the struggle with the wind. This being so, they were glad enough to accept the light-keeper's kind invitation.

Peggy's first action, however, was to hasten to the 'phone in the lighthouse and call up their aunt. Miss Prescott, who had been badly worried over their prolonged absence, was much relieved to learn that they were safe and sound.

Mrs. Beasley, a motherly woman of middle age, took charge of Peggy while Jeff Stokes entertained Roy. Jeff said that he liked the life at the light, lonesome as it grew sometimes. When he felt blue he used to relieve the monotony by talking, by means of invisible waves, with other operators. He wiled many a weary hour away in this manner, he said.

Suddenly, in the midst of their talk, he excused himself and hastened to the small room in which his instruments were. The place, filled with shiny, mysterious apparatus and networked above with wires, was as neat as a pin.

"Some one's calling," Jeff explained.

His quick ear had caught the faint "tick-tick" hardly audible to the untrained ears, which told him that a message was vibrating through the night. Slipping over his head a metallic apparatus, not unlike the telephone receivers worn by "Central," Jeff began listening intently.

Drawing a pad toward him, he was soon writing down the message as it was ticked off. Presently it was completed, by which time Peggy was one of his audience.

"'Steamer Valiant, Captain Briggs, of London, wishes to be reported as passing Rocky Point, bound for Boston,'" read off Jeff. "Hum — nothing very exciting there."

"What are you going to do now?" asked Peggy, as Jeff, the message in his hand, turned to another table, one on which were arranged some ordinary telegraph instruments.

"Send it by ordinary wire telegraphy into the head office in New York," he said.

"Why not send it by wireless?" asked Peggy.

"Too much chance of delay and getting cross currents," explained Jeff. "We found that for quick transmission of ordinary business, that the wire is best, unless the atmospheric conditions are just right."

Suddenly, one of the telegraph instruments began to crackle and click loudly.

"Phew!" said Jeff, listening intently; "here's something that will interest you folks."

"What is it?" asked Peggy, eagerly.

"It's — wait a minute till I catch the last—" Jeff listened a few seconds more and then faced about. "Why, that message was a despatch from the Sandy Bay correspondent of the New York Planet to his paper," he said. "It was an article telling that Fanning Harding has completed a successful aeroplane which made a wonderful flight to-night in a stiff wind. He says that Harding has formed a company and means to manufacture similar craft. Then there was a lot of taffy about what a fine young fellow Harding is, and how bright, and so on. Wonder if it's true?"

"I can vouch for that," said Peggy. "I've seen his factory. It's out by Gid Gibbons's shop."

"So that's where Gid is getting all his money," exclaimed Jeff. "I saw him spending it like water in Sandy Bay the other day. Hester's got a lot of new dresses and hats, too."

Peggy's heart beat a little faster. This sounded like a corroboration of her suspicions. Where could such a man as Gid Gibbons be getting such large amounts of money as he seemed to have recently? But before she could ask any more questions Mrs. Beasley announced supper. Speculation was rife in Peggy's mind as they sat down to the broiled sea bass, freshly caught, home-grown potatoes and string beans and other good things which the light-keeper had designated as "rough fare." Peggy was fain to admit afterward, and so was Roy, that never had she enjoyed anything so much as that meal in the old lighthouse with the wind roaring about it and the rough, kindly faces of their entertainers smiling on them.

Good-natured Mrs. Beasley soon after arranged sleeping accommodations for her young guests, and that night the young aviators slumbered peacefully, while above them the great revolving light swept steadily in slow circles, warning vessels passing up and down the Sound of the dangerous proximity of Rocky Point.

The next day dawned bright and fair. The sea lay like a sheet of blue glass, with scarcely a ripple to mar its polished surface. The last trace of the wind had died down.

"We'll have no more breeze till sundown," announced Mr. Beasley at breakfast. Like most men of his profession, he was an earnest and accurate student of the weather. After breakfast Jeff Stokes, who had been on duty all night, was relieved by his assistant, a young man who boarded in the village and rode over to his duty on a motor-cycle.

"Well," said Roy, after they had thanked their good-hearted entertainers warmly, "I guess it's time for us to be getting home."

But Peggy had noted a wistful look in Jeff Stokes's eyes as he stood by the side of the aeroplane, which an examination had already shown to be none the worse for its buffeting of the night before.

"Would you like to try a little flight, Jeff?" she asked.

"Would I?" echoed the youth; "will a duck swim?"

"Yes, I believe so," laughed Roy, "and so can a certain young wireless operator fly."

"Gee, Roy, you mean it?"

"Of course, if you're not scared."

There was a mischievous twinkle in Roy's eye as he bent over the engine.

"How would you like a ride, Mr. Beasley?" asked Peggy presently, while Roy adjusted the engine.

The weather-beaten old fellow fairly threw up his hands.

"Land of Goshen, miss!" he exclaimed, "I've lived on the earth and sea, man and boy, for fifty years, and I ain't agoin' ter tempt Providence by embarking in a sky clipper at this late day."

"You bet you ain't," put in Mrs. Beasley with deep conviction. "Why, if you ever done such a thing we'd be like to be read out of church—not but what it's all right for young folks if they know how to manage the contraptions."

"Now, then, Jeff, if you are ready will you get in?" said Roy presently.

The slender young wireless operator hopped into the chassis with alacrity. But his face was a bit pallid from excitement at the idea of the new method of locomotion he was about to test.

Last good-byes were said, and the motor began to whirr like a gigantic locust. There was a grinding and buzzing as the gears meshed and the aeroplane began to scud off.

"Fer all ther world like some big, pesky grasshopper," declared Mrs. Beasley, as it scudded off across the smooth turf.

But if the good lady was astonished, then it was nothing to her amazement when a moment later the Butterfly soared up into the air, lifting as gently on the windless atmosphere as a bit of drifting gossamer.

Up and up it swept in graceful hawk-like circles.

"Dear Suz!" shrieked Mrs. Beasley presently, "if they ain't agoin' out ter sea!"

"Just what they air," shouted her husband, shading his eyes with a wrinkled hand. "I never thought ter have lived ter have seen such a thing!"

Roy had been unable to resist the temptation to take a little spin out above the glassy, scarcely heaving water. The gulls, soaring above it, viewed with amazement the invasion of their realm by this buzzing, angry looking monster. They flew about it shrieking.

"Goodness, I hope they don't attack us," exclaimed Peggy.

"Not likely," was Roy's response. "They think we are some kind of big bird, I guess, and want to have a game with us."

As they swept on, all agreed that never had they felt such a feeling of exhilaration as came to them as they swooped and swung above the glistening blue water, for all the world like some huge bird. Once or twice motor boats went by beneath them, and the occupants looked up at first in wonderment and then in enthusiasm at the sight the Golden Butterfly and her three young occupants presented.

But all at once the steady song of the engine began to grow different. It "skipped" and sputtered and coughed. Blue smoke rolled from the exhausts. The aeroplane began to waver and sag.

Jeff Stokes turned rather pale.

"What is the matter?" he gasped, steadying his voice as much as he could as the aeroplane began to drop steadily down toward the water beneath them.

"The gasolene's given out," rejoined Roy in a voice which was full of anxiety.

"Oh, Roy, what shall we do?"

Peggy gasped as the aeroplane, its propeller beating the air more and more feebly, began to descend with greater rapidity.

"We'll have to volplane to some land if we can, and if we can't we must take our chances for it in the water," was Roy's grim reply.

CHAPTER XII.
WHAT HAPPENED ON THE ISLAND.

"Look," cried Peggy suddenly, "isn't that a small island below there? Maybe we can make that?"

"I'll try to," was the answer, as Roy gripped the steering wheel more firmly.

At the same instant the motor, with a gasp and a sputter, gave out altogether. But Roy knew how to volplane; that is, to reach the earth by swinging the aeroplane in circles so that her stability was maintained even with the power cut off.

He began to execute this maneuver now. The island which Peggy had indicated was a small spot of land some five miles off the shore. It was sandy and barren looking on one side, though at the further end from them there grew some trees and scrubby looking bushes.

If he could only keep the aeroplane from sagging down into the sea Roy was confident he could land at the place in safety. But it was still some distance off and the aeroplane was still dropping with much greater rapidity than seemed comfortable. Both Roy and his sister were expert swimmers, and the boy knew that Jeff was at home in the water. But at the same time, if they struck the surface of the sea, there was the chance that they might become entangled in the aeroplane and drowned before they had an opportunity to save themselves. So it was with a keen sense of apprehension that the boy exercised all the air craft of which he was master in bringing his sky cruiser downward.

"Oh!" cried Peggy suddenly as the Golden Butterfly gave a sickening downward drop like a stone plunging to vacancy.

But the empty "air pocket" which the craft had struck was a small one, and the next instant the atmosphere caught the broad wings and buoyed the aeroplane up from what seemed to be destined to be a disastrous fall.

The drop had, however, had one good effect. It had thrown the aeroplane almost on end, and in that manner drained a few last driblets of gasolene from the depleted tank into the feed pipes.

It was only a little fuel, but it was enough to cause the engine to resume operations for a couple of minutes. Taking advantage of this lucky accident, Roy drove forward, and as the propeller came once more to a standstill the Golden Butterfly sank down into a bed of sand which made her almost at once stationary.

"Well, we are—aerial Robinson Crusoes," exclaimed Peggy as, having clambered out of the chassis, she stood surveying the little island which they had so fortunately landed upon.

"Yes, and if we don't get some gasolene pretty quick we'll be Crusoes in a mighty uncomfortable sense," commented Roy, moodily gazing about at the surrounding sea, smooth as a sheet of glass and without the sign of a boat upon it. Far off on the horizon there hung a three-masted schooner, all her sails set, in the flat calm. But she was too far off to aid them even had she been able to.

"Tell you what we'll do, let's explore the island," said Jeff Stokes suddenly.

"Of course," cried Peggy, clapping her hands, "that's what everybody does in story books when they are stranded on a desert island, and right after that they always find just what they want, even down to a silver-mounted manicure set."

"I'd like to see a tin-mounted can of gasolene," grunted Roy. Nevertheless after seeing to the engine of the aeroplane he was willing enough to set out with the others to explore this little spot of land in the Sound.

It was so small that it did not take them long to reach the summit of the low peak into which it rose in the centre.

"Oh, there's a little hut!" cried Peggy, suddenly.

Sure enough, below them, and half overgrown with tall weeds and scrub growth, was a half ruined hut. It was doubtless the relic of some fisherman who had once used the island as headquarters. But it had, apparently, long lapsed into disuse.

Hardly had they spied it before Roy made another discovery. Drawn up in a miniature cove not far from the hut was a trim and trig white motor boat, seemingly, from her long narrow shape and powerful engines, capable of great speed.

Here was a discovery! A motor boat meant gasolene and companionship.

With a soft cry of joy Peggy was dashing forward toward the hut, from which they could now hear proceeding the hum of human voices, when Roy suddenly checked her. From the doorway there had suddenly issued the figure of Morgan, the Bancrofts' butler. He gazed about him with a look of half alarmed suspicion on his flabby face. The young aviators instinctively crouched back behind a screen of green brush. They felt a suddenly aroused premonition that everything was not as it should be.

"H'its nothink," said Morgan, addressing someone within the hut, after he had gazed about a little more without seeing anything to further alarm his suspicions.

"All right, if that's the case come back in here," came another voice from inside the hut.

"Giles!" recognized the astonished Peggy. But another and a greater surprise was yet in store for them when they heard another voice strike into the conversation. There was no mistaking the tones for any others than Fanning Harding's.

"You chaps are nervous as kittens," he was saying, "who on earth would come to this island? We are as private here as if we were in the South Seas. Now go ahead, Morgan, with what you were saying."

"Well, what h'I says is this," spoke up the English butler, "a fair diwision and no favoritism. You say you want a third? You ain't h'entitled to h'it. H'it was h'only by h'accident that you found h'out h'our secret h'and h'I thinks you ought to be content with what you can get."

"Very well," was the rejoinder, "but as you fellows know, I've got you in my power. You daren't make a move without consulting me. If you try any monkey tricks I'll crush you so quick you won't know what struck you. The police are still carrying on their investigation, and—"

But here the voices sank so low that the eager young listeners could hear no more. But their eyes shone as they exchanged glances. Somehow both Peggy and Roy felt that the conversation had related to the mysterious vanishing of the jewels. This at least appeared clear from Fanning Harding's reference to the police.

"We'd better get back to the other side of the island before they come out and see us," counseled Peggy. "If they were to find out we had been spying on them they might get frightened and spirit the jewels away from wherever they have them concealed, for I'm just as sure now that they are all three mixed up in it as I am that—that—"

"We have no gasolene," put in Roy.

"But you have no proof and nothing to go upon," objected Jeff Stokes who was, like most folks around Sandy Bay, familiar with the details of the strange occurrence.

"That's just the trouble," said Peggy, "and it is just as impossible to go ahead in the case as it is for us to fly without fuel."

"Peg!" cried Roy, suddenly, "look at that!"

"That" was a ten gallon can of gasolene standing on the beach by the side of the motor boat. Evidently, to drag her bow up on the beach, they had lightened the craft so as to make the task easier, for several ropes, water jars and other bits of marine tackle lay about.

"If we could only get it," sighed Peggy.

"Yes, if," was the rejoinder from Roy, "but we can't steal it, and, as you say, it might spoil everything if Fanning Harding thought that we had overheard any of his talk."

"Look out!" warned Jeff Stokes in a whisper the next instant. The warning did not come a bit too soon. The door of the hut opened and the party which had been in conference inside emerged. They made straight for the motor boat, which Jeff Stokes had, in the meantime, recognized as one that was for hire at Sandy Bay.

"Come on, boys, we've got to be getting back," urged Fanning moving quickly and preparing to shove the craft off.

"Wait till I chuck some of this truck in," grumbled Giles.

He stooped and rapidly threw in the ropes and other gear scattered about. Then as Fanning Harding and the flabby-faced butler shoved the craft off he made a hasty scramble for the boat's bow, leaping in as she floated free of the beach.

"H'I soy," shouted Morgan, "you forgot the bloomin' gasolene."

"Better put back and get it," growled Giles; "if you fellows had helped me a bit instead of givin' advice it wouldn't have bin forgotten."

"Oh, we can't bother with it now," struck in Fanning, impatiently, "we've plenty in the tank to take us back. I'm not going to delay any longer."

He spun over the fly wheel as he spoke and the motor boat began to cut rapidly through the water headed for Sandy Bay. As soon as it had gone a safe distance the three stranded young adventurers joined hands and executed a wild war dance of joy. By a means almost miraculous they had fallen across the very thing they needed.

"It's just like the story books!" cried Peggy, delightedly.

They raced down toward the coveted can, which was half full of the precious fuel. Enough to get them ashore at any rate. Before returning to the stranded aeroplane they examined the hut, but found nothing in it but a few broken-down bits of furniture.

"Queer," commented Jeff, "I half expected to find something."

"Not likely," laughed Roy, "they're too foxy for that."

"What do you suppose they came to the island for?" asked Peggy.

"To get a quiet place to talk where they would not be observed by any one who knew them, I guess," rejoined her brother. "Oh, if only we could solve the mystery. It's tantalizing to be so close to it and yet with so many tangled ends left ravelled."

"Be patient," advised Peggy, "it will all come out in time. And now I'm as famished for lunch as the Golden Butterfly is, so lets fill up the tank and then head for home."

"Second the motion," laughed Jeff Stokes.

Half an hour later the Golden Butterfly once more rose, and without incident or mishap winged her way back to Rocky Point.

CHAPTER XIII.
JUKES DADE APPEARS.

The aviation field at Acatonick a few days before the big contests for juvenile aviators was alive with action and color. The spot selected was a flat, smooth field of some fifty acres on the outskirts of the town.

The grass spread a green carpet, thickly sprinkled with wild flowers, while at one side of the place was a row of green-painted sheds known as the "hangars."

"Hangar is French for shed," Peggy had explained to a group of friends from Sandy Bay whom she was showing over the grounds, "and I think that shed is a whole lot better word than 'Ongar,' which is the way you are supposed to pronounce it."

One of the sheds—as in deference to Peggy we shall call them—was of a different color, and stood somewhat apart from the rest. It was also much larger and bore in consequential-looking letters over its door the words:

"Harding Aeroplane Company. Keep Out."

And to see that this notice was enforced to the letter, Fanning Harding had installed a red-nosed watchman with a formidable club at the portal. Considerable secrecy, in fact, had been observed concerning his aeroplane. Several large boxes had arrived one night and been hustled as quickly as possible into the shed.

The shed assigned to Roy Prescott, happened, by an odd coincidence, to be next door to the Harding one. The second day of their stay at Acatonick, Roy, on coming down to the field from the hotel at which he and Peggy and Miss Prescott were stopping, was much surprised to be greeted by Fanning, with some effusiveness.

After a lot of preliminary hemming and hawing, Fanning broached to Roy once more the proposition of selling the Golden Butterfly.

"But I thought you had a fine type of aeroplane of your own," said Roy, wondering at this renewal of Fanning's offer.

"So I have," was the rejoinder, "but now that I have established my business on a paying business basis I can handle another type. You know mine is a biplane model."

Roy nodded. He had no liking for Fanning, but the other was so effusive that he felt it was incumbent on him to meet the other lad half way, as the saying is.

"I'd like to have a look at your craft sometime," he said.

"Not much you won't," rejoined Fanning, quickly, "you'll see her on the day she wins the big prize and not before."

"You seem to have it won already," rejoined Roy, rather contemptuously.

"Oh, yes," was the confident reply, "I'm going to simply fly rings round you and the rest, so you'd better take up my offer now, for after the race your Golden Butterfly stock won't be worth a penny."

"I'm not so certain about that," was the answer.

"Then you won't take up my offer. I'll raise it another two hundred."

Roy smiled and shook his head. Something in his refusal angered the other lad.

"Well as you wish," he said, strolling off, "but dad has been pretty lenient with you up to date. As you won't meet us half way, though I'm going to advise him to force you to sell the Golden Butterfly."

"How?"

"By foreclosing that mortgage without further delay."

Fanning whipped the words out with a vicious intonation. All his mean nature surged up into his face as he spoke. Roy breathed a little quicker. But outwardly he was calm and cold as ice.

"That's your privilege," he said shortly, turning away, but that night he and Peggy had a troubled discussion about ways and means, and it became more than ever evident to them how much depended on winning the five thousand dollar prize.

There were several aspirants in the juvenile class on the grounds as well as fliers of more mature years, for Mr. Higgins had interested some other capitalists, and it had been decided to make quite an event out of the aerial meet.

On the day before the race, which meant so much to them, Peggy and Roy decided to take a practice spin across country in their 'plane. The capable looking machine excited much favorable comment when it was wheeled out of its shed. Several of the other competitors gathered about it while the engine was being tuned up. Among them was a surly looking chap with a dark, roughly-shaven chin and a pair of shifty eyes. He stood beside Fanning Harding, who was also in the crowd about the Golden Butterfly.

The Sandy Bay boy gazed on with a sneering look while our two young aviators got everything in readiness. This took some time for everybody was anxious to take a hand in the work, and it was quite a task to kindly, but steadfastly, reject these offers, well meant as they were.

At last everything appeared to be in good shape and with a buzz and a whirr the engine was tried out. It worked perfectly, and before the crowd had had time to cheer, the aeroplane shot up from the ground in front of its shed with hardly any preliminary run. Then came a belated cheer.

"That's the craft that wins the big prize," said a stout, good-natured looking man.

"Don't you be so certain," snapped out Fanning Harding, who stood close by, and to whom the words were gall.

"Why, what's the matter with you, my young friend," asked the jovial man; "you must be meaning to get it yourself."

"That's right," was the confident reply.

"Well, don't count your aerial chicks before they're hatched," was the merry rejoinder. A laugh at Fanning's expense went up from the crowd. The boy flushed angrily and strode off in the direction of his hangar.

"Confound that young Jackanapes of a Roy Prescott," he muttered, as he went; "he gets ahead of me every time. But I'll fix him. Pop needs that land, and if Roy wins this race the Prescotts can pay off that mortgage and be on the road to riches. Well, I guess I'll settle all that. But I'll have to act quickly."

"You seem to be sore on that Prescott boy," came a voice at his shoulder suddenly.

Fanning turned quickly to find himself confronted by the unprepossessing individual who had stood at his side during the start of the Golden Butterfly, which was by this time almost out of sight in the eastward.

"Why, what do you know about it?" he asked, sharply.

"Well," was the rejoinder, "being an observing sort of an individual I figured out that you were not best pleased at seeing what a fine aeroplane that kid has. Right, ain't I?"

He coolly took from his pocket a disgusting-looking cigar stump and proceeded to light it, leering impudently into Fanning's face the while.

"Well, may be you are and then again you may not be," was the Sandy Bay youngster's cautious reply; "but how does it interest you?"

"Because I haven't any more use for him than you have, and if you make it worth my while I'll give you a bit of information that will be of value to you."

"What do you mean?" inquired Fanning, beginning to listen with more attention than he had hitherto shown.

"Just this, that I'm Jukes Dade, who used to work for Mr. Prescott years ago, but he discharged me for—for—well for a little fault of drinking I had. Come now, don't you recognize me?"

"By George, I do," exclaimed Fanning; "but it was so many years ago you were with Mr. Prescott that I hardly knew you. You have changed greatly."

"I may have," was the reply in bitter tones. "I've been through enough. But there's one thing I ain't never forgotten in all these years, and that is my resolve to get even on old man Prescott."

"But he is dead," put in Fanning, wondering at the baleful expression of hatred that had come into the man's face.

"All true enough. I heard that some time ago. But if I can injure the son in any way, I'd like to do it. I've got a wrong to avenge, and if you want to pay well to have Roy Prescott put out of the race to-morrow I'm your man."

"Hush, don't talk so loud. Some folks over there are looking at us."

"Oh, well, if you're afraid to—"

"No, no, that isn't it. I must prevent Roy winning that race tomorrow at all hazards. Come into my hangar and we can talk quietly."

"Ah, that's the talk," was the rejoinder, and Jukes Dade chuckled with grim delight. "You want a little job of work done to settle our friend's hash. Well, you've come to the right shop when you meet up with old Jukes Dade who has an axe of his own to grind."

CHAPTER XIV.
A GIRL AVIATOR'S ADVENTURE.

In the meantime, Peggy and Roy, the former at the steering wheel and controls, were skimming through the air above the charming country surrounding Acatonick. The exhilaration of flying, the thrill and zest of it, were strong upon them as they glided along, and they made an extended flight.

"She is working like a three-hundred-dollar watch," cried Roy joyously as the speedy monoplane flew onward.

"She's a darling," was Peggy's enthusiastic response. "I'm sure that if nothing happens you'll win that race to-morrow, Roy."

"I hope so, little sister," was the response, "for there's a whole lot depending on it."

"But just think. If you only do we shall be at the end of our troubles."

"Not quite, sis," Roy reminded her, "that affair of the missing jewels is still a mystery, and as long as it stays so some folks will always be suspicious of me."

"Oh, Roy, don't say such things. Nobody but the horridest of the horrid would—"

"Unluckily," struck in the boy, "there are a lot of the horridest of the horrid in this world, and some of them are in Sandy Bay."

He laughed and then went on more seriously:

"It's a pretty nasty feeling, I can tell you, to know that you are unjustly suspected by several folks of—of—er—knowing more about an affair of that kind than you tell."

"What can have become of the jewels?"

"Ah, that's just it. Of course we have our suspicion, based really on nothing, that Fanning Harding knows something about them. But if he did why would he place that wallet on the porch of Jess's home?"

"It's beyond me."

"And beyond me, too. I'm quite sure that nobody was about the place when the accident happened, and I could not have been unconscious more than a few seconds. Now who could have stolen the wallet in that time?"

"It will all come out in time. I'm sure of it, Roy, dear," said Peggy, earnestly. "Perhaps it will turn out to be not such a mystery after all."

"I don't know," was Roy's rejoinder. "Mr. Bancroft has had some of the cleverest detectives in the country on the case, and a description of the jewels, some of which were heirlooms, has been wired everywhere broadcast. But up to date none of them have turned up at any pawnshops or other likely places."

For some moments more they talked in this strain, when Peggy suddenly gave a cry and pointed below. They were passing over a tiny lake surrounded by steeply sloping banks, wooded with beautiful trees. It was an isolated spot, no human habitation being near at hand apparently.

"Oh, isn't that pretty?" cried Peggy delightedly. "It looks as if it might have come out of a picture book."

"And the sight of that water reminds me that I'm terribly thirsty," said Roy. "I bet there are some springs by that lake, or if there are not maybe the water is good to drink from the lake itself."

"Let's go down and see," said Peggy, with a bright smile, and setting over a lever and twisting a couple of valves she began to depress the aeroplane.

"There's a good landing place off there to the right of the end of the lake," cried Roy, indicating a bare spot where some land seemed to have been cleared at one time.

"All right, my brilliant brother," laughed Peggy merrily. "I saw it at least five minutes ago. Hold tight, I'm going to drop fast."

To any one less accustomed to aerial navigation than our two young friends, the downward plunge would have been alarming in its velocity. But to them it was merely exciting. Within a few feet of the ground, just when it seemed they must dash against the surface of the earth with crushing force, Peggy set the planes on a rising angle and the Golden Eagle settled to earth as gracefully as a tired bird.

"Well, here we are," exclaimed Roy, looking about him at the sylvan scene as they alighted; "and now what comes next?"

"A hunt for the spring, of course," cried Peggy, placing one hand on her brother's shoulder and nimbly leaping from the chassis to the soft, springy ground. And off they set toward the margin of the little lake below them.

"Reminds me of Ponce de Leon's hunt for a spring," laughed Roy, who felt in high spirits over the fine way the Golden Butterfly had conducted herself.

"But he was looking for the Fountain of Eternal Youth," said Peggy, quickly.

"Wonder if he'd have been any happier if he'd found it," murmured Roy, philosophically.

"If he'd been a woman he would," said Peggy.

"Would what? Have found it?"

"No, you goose, but have been perfectly happy if he had attained perpetual youth. Why, I think—Why, whatever was that?"

The girl broke off short in her laughing remarks and an expression of startled astonishment crept over her features.

"Why, it's some one groaning," cried Roy, after a brief period of listening.

"Yes. Some one in pain, too. It's off this way. Come on, Roy, let us find out what is the matter."

Without a thought of personal danger, but with all her warm girlish sympathy aroused, plucky Peggy plunged off on to a path, from a spot along which it appeared the injured person must be groaning. But Roy caught her arm and pulled her back while he stepped in front of her.

"Let me go first, sis," he said; "we don't know what may be the matter."

Peggy dutifully tiptoed along behind, as with hearts that beat somewhat faster than usual they made their way down the narrow path which led them into the deep gloom of the deeper woods. All at once Roy halted. They had arrived on the edge of a little clearing in the midst of which stood a tiny and roughly built hut with a big stone chimney at one end. Although the place was primitive it was scrupulously neat.

Painted white with green shutters, with a bright flower garden in front, it was a veritable picture of rural thrift.

The boy hesitated for an instant as they stood on the opposite edge of the cleared ground. There was no question but that they had reached the place whence the groans had proceeded. As they stood there the grim sounds began once more, after being hushed for an instant. Now, however, they took coherent form.

"Oh, help me! Help me!"

Roy was undetermined no longer. Directing Peggy to remain outside till he summoned her, he walked rapidly, and with a firm step, up the path leading to the hut, and entered. It was so dark inside that at first he could see nothing. But pretty soon he spied a huddled form in one corner.

"Oh, don't hurt me! I'm only a harmless old man! I have no money," cried the cringing figure, as Roy entered.

"I don't want to hurt you," said the boy kindly; "I want to help you."

He now saw that the form in the corner was that of an old man with a silvery beard and long white hair. From a gash on his forehead blood was flowing, and the wound seemed to have been recently inflicted.

"What is the matter? What has happened?" asked Roy, gently, as he raised the old man to a chair into which he fell limply.

"Water! water!" he cried, feebly.

Roy hastened outside saying to himself as he went:

"This is a case for Peggy."

Summoning her he hastily related what had occurred and the warm-hearted girl, with many exclamations of pity, hastened to the wounded man's side.

"Get me some water quick, Roy," she exclaimed, tearing a long strip from her linen petticoat to serve as a bandage. Outside the hut,

Roy soon found a spring, back of a rickety stable in which the old man had a horse and a ramshackle buggy.

When he returned with the water the poor old fellow took a long draught from a cup Peggy held to his lips and the girl then deftly washed and bandaged his wound. This done the venerable old man seemed to rally, and sitting up in his chair thanked his young friends warmly. Roy, in the meantime, had been looking about the hut and saw that it was furnished in plain, but tidy style. Over the great open fireplace, at one end, hung a big picture. Evidently the canvas was many years old. It was the portrait of a fine, self-reliant looking young man in early manhood. His blue eyes gazed confidently out from the picture and a smile of seeming satisfaction quivered about his lips.

"I'll bet that's a fellow who has got on in the world," thought Roy to himself as he scanned the capable, strong features.

"Ah," said the old man, observing the lad's interest in the painting, "that picture is a relic of old, old days. It is a portrait of my brother James. He—But I must tell you how I came to be in the sad condition in which you found me. Have you a comfortable chair, miss? Yes, very well, then I will tell you what happened this afternoon in this hut, and will then relate to you something of my own story for I was not always a hermit and an outcast."

CHAPTER XV.
THE HERMIT OF THE WOODS.

"My name is Peter Bell," began the old man, "and many years ago I was like any other happy, care-free young man, who is the son of well-to-do parents. I had a brother named James Bell, who was much younger than me. We were very fond of each other and inseparable.

"Our home was on the Long Island coast and we often went boating. One day when we were out in my boat a storm came up and she capsized. I tried to save my brother who was a poor swimmer. But in the midst of my efforts the bulwark of the wave-tossed boat struck my head and rendered me insensible. It seems, however, I must have clung to the boat, for when I came to myself I had almost been blown ashore, and, striking out, I soon reached it.

"But to my horror I soon saw that people shunned me. In some way the story got about that I had saved myself at the expense of my brother's life. Such stories are always readily credited among the majority of people in a small town and the tale spread like wildfire with exaggerations. Driven half wild by the general contempt which I met on every side I left home one night, and having a sum of money in my own right I decided to live the life of a recluse.

"I recollected this spot to which I had come on hunting expeditions in brighter days. Not long after, grief over my brother's death resulted in my mother's life coming to a close, and shortly afterward my father's demise occurred.

"They left but little, but I managed to secure that portrait of my brother you see hanging up there and a few bits of favorite furniture associated with happier times.

"I have lived here ever since and have become reconciled to my fate. From time to time I used to advertise for news of my brother, offering rewards, but long ago I stopped that, and have no doubt that he perished in the storm, although for a time I comforted myself by thinking that he might, by some strange chance, have been saved.

"In some way a rumor has spread through the countryside that I have much wealth hidden here, and this afternoon four masked men entered the hut and when I protested, in reply to their demands, that I had no money, they struck me down and searched the house. Then cursing me for a fraud and an impostor because they found no gold they left, leaving me to my fate."

"You have no idea who the men were?" asked Roy who, like Peggy, had listened with close attention to the old man's story.

"Yes, I think they were young men of bad reputation from a neighboring village; however, I am not sure. I am certain that I recollected hearing the voice of one of them when I was in the market in that village some time ago."

"Oh, then, you do go into town sometimes?" asked Roy.

"Oh, yes," rejoined the hermit, "but no more than I can help. I have long since departed from the ways of the world and the habitations of men. But I gather herbs in the woods for miles about and sell them to folks in the villages."

"I suppose that is why you have the horse and cart?" put in Peggy, who had been gazing out of the window and had noticed the tumbledown barn.

"Yes," rejoined the old man. "I am not as active as I was once and my old bones will not carry me as far as they used to. So I drive old Dobbin when I have a journey of any length to make."

The hermit would not hear of any help being summoned for him. He said that he was in no danger of a second attack, as the search of his little property had been thorough and had resulted in the rascals, who had invaded his haunts, getting nothing for their pains. Refusing some refreshment the old man offered, the young aviators soon after left the hut, promising to call in again in a few days and give the hermit an opportunity to see the aeroplane in which he was much interested. The old man asked them many questions about the races of the next day and seemed interested in hearing the details.

The Golden Butterfly they found just as they had left her, and clambering on board they were soon winging their way back to

Acatonick where, as you may imagine, they had an interesting story of the incidents of the afternoon to relate to Miss Prescott that evening.

"I never saw such children for adventures in all my born days," she declared, "but I have a letter here which I must show you. I am afraid it means that we shall have to leave the old home."

She drew an envelope from her handbag which lay on a table of the hotel room and handed it to Roy. On opening it, he found that it contained a formal notice from the Sandy Bay Bank, that unless the accumulated interest and other moneys owing them were paid up within a week that foreclosure proceedings would be taken. The boy gave a disconsolate whistle as he finished reading the letter aloud and handed it back.

He had hardly done so when there came a rap on the door of the room. "I wonder who that can be so late?" thought Roy, getting up and going to the door.

A bellboy stood there with a note.

"A messenger just brought this from the aviation grounds," he said. "Any answer?"

"Wait a minute," said Roy, skimming hastily through the note. It was typewritten and signed:—James Jarvis, Superintendent of Arrangements.

"Dear sir: You are requested to report at the executive tent at once. An important meeting will take place affecting the competitors in the races to-morrow."

This was what Roy read. Then he turned to the bellboy and told the lad to inform the messenger that he would be there as soon as possible.

"Queer though," he said to Peggy and his aunt. "I didn't know of any meeting that was scheduled to take place to-night. I guess it's one that's been called at the eleventh hour to make some arrangements."

"That must be it," agreed Peggy. "Shall I come with you?"

"No, thanks, sis," rejoined the boy; "you'd better get to bed. It's going to be an exciting day to-morrow for us all."

The boy snatched up his cap and with a hasty good-bye, was off.

Downstairs in the lobby of the hotel he found the messenger awaiting him,—a shifty-eyed man with a blue chin. It was, in fact,

Jukes Dade, who, in a different suit of clothes and with a clean shave and haircut, looked a trifle more presentable than he had earlier in the day when he made himself known to Fanning.

"This way, sir," he said, with a fawning sort of bow.

"Out of this door is the quickest," said Roy quickly, with a feeling that he would rather walk to the grounds alone than with such a companion.

"But we're not going to walk, sir. The committee has sent an auto for you."

"A car, eh?" said Roy; "well, that's considerate of them. I'll tell my sister. She might like to come along, too."

The messenger shook his head.

"Sorry, sir; but we've got to pick up some other aviators on our way and every bit of room in the car will be taken."

"Oh, very well, then," said Roy, "lead on."

The blue-chinned Dade shuffled across the lobby with a furtive air.

"Funny," thought Roy. "I've seen that chap some place before, but to save my life I can't place him."

Cudgelling his brains to try to recall where he had met the man, Roy passed through the hotel lobby and out into the street. In the lamplight he saw a big car standing at the curb, shaking as its ungeared engine puffed and chugged. A chauffeur, with an auto mask and goggles on, sat on the front seat. Roy got in behind in the tonneau while the messenger took his seat by the chauffeur.

He said something in a low whisper to the driver and the next instant there was a grinding whirr as the gears were connected and the car rolled forward.

"Well, they've got a good fast car here," thought Roy, as the machine sped along over the roads. "At this rate we ought to be at the grounds in—"

But what was this? Surely the road they were on was not the right one. Leaning forward he touched the chauffeur on the shoulder.

"This isn't the road to the grounds," he said.

"Oh, yes it is," put in the messenger; "it's a short cut, though. Isn't it, Fred?"

The chauffeur did not speak but merely nodded his head.

Although by no means satisfied with the explanation, Roy made no immediate comment. In the meantime they had passed the outskirts of the little town and were now whizzing along an unlighted road bordered with big trees. On and on they went, and Roy, every minute, grew more uneasy. Where could they be taking him?

"Where are you going?" he demanded suddenly, his suspicion showing in his tone as he rose in the tonneau and leaned forward. "I want you to know that—"

But before he could utter another word the blue-chinned messenger did an astonishing thing. With a quick, imperceptible movement he produced a revolver and thrust its gleaming barrel up under Roy's nose.

"Sit back and keep quiet," he warned, "and you'll be all right. If you make a holler you'll get what's in this barker."

As he spoke the auto began to slow down, and presently a dark form stepped from the shadows of the trees ahead and stood awaiting its coming.

CHAPTER XVI.
THE ENEMY'S MOVE.

Roy's first feeling was one of indignation at the fellow's impudence.

"What do you mean by such conduct," he blurted out angrily. "Take me to the aviation grounds at once, or—"

"That's just where we are taking you away from, young fellow," sneered the man behind the pistol. "Ah! Don't move. I'm very nervous and if I get excited this pistol might go off. It's very light on the trigger."

As he spoke the auto slowed down almost to a standstill, and the man who had evidently been waiting for it, swung himself on the running board and joined the others on the front seat. Like the driver, he wore a motoring mask and goggles which effectively concealed his features, and yet to Roy there was something familiar even about the muffled up figure. Once the third man was aboard, the auto plunged forward once more at breakneck speed. It rocked from side to side on the rough road as it flew along. But the man with the pistol kept his weapon levelled at Roy throughout all its jouncings and joltings.

Like a wise boy, Roy had concluded that it would be worse than foolish to attempt any resistance to his abductors. So he sat motionless and silent as the car tore onward through the night. He had not the least idea where they were, nor for what place they could be bound. Nor had he yet had time to think over the reason for this bold kidnapping.

Now, however, it was plain that the object of the trip was to take him to some place and hold him prisoner till the aero race was over. It struck him with cruel force that, unless he could manage to escape, the object of the expedition seemed very likely to prove successful.

All at once the car struck a bump in the road with a violent wrenching thud. It leaped into the air like a live thing while a frightened shout burst from the throats of the men on the front seat.

Mechanically Roy gripped the sides of the tonneau to avoid being thrown out like a missile.

The next instant, with a rasping grind and a sickening swaying and jouncing the car tore full tilt down the side of the road, which, at this point, was banked, and fetched up motionless and hub-deep in a pool of dark water.

"Don't let the kid escape," came a shout from the man who had boarded the car on the roadside, as the auto ceased to move.

But before the words had left his lips Roy had perceived that the water in the pond was not much more than knee high. Quick as a cat he was out of the tonneau before any of the others had time to collect their wits. As the man shouted his warning the lad struck out through the oozy ground, seeking, with every ounce of his strength, to shroud himself in the darkness at the pond edge before the pistol wielder could locate him.

But he had not gone more than a few steps when—

Bang!

A red flash cut the night behind him and a bullet whistled by his ear.

"Look out, you fool, you don't want to kill him," came a voice behind him.

"Gid Gibbons," flashed through Roy's mind. He was almost at a thick clump of alders now. As he heard the splashing of the bodies of the abductors, as they took to the water after him, he plunged into the coppice and pushed rapidly on into its intricacies.

Shouts and cries came from behind him, and suddenly a blinding shaft of white radiance cut through the blackness. They had turned on the searchlight of the car in a determined effort to locate their escaped prisoner.

As the light penetrated among the maze of alder trunks, Roy threw himself flat. While his pursuers hunted about, muttering and angrily discussing the situation, he crouched in his shelter, hardly daring to breathe. After what seemed an eternity of suspense he heard one of the men, whose voice he seemed to recognize as that of the pistol carrier, angrily declaiming.

"Aw, what's ther use, ther kid is a mile off by this time, worse luck."

"Hush, don't talk so loud," came another voice. "You don't know who may be about."

"Well, we'd better be getting that car out of the mud and making ourselves scarce," came in the tones which Roy was certain were those of Gid Gibbons. "If there's a hue and cry raised about this and they find that car stranded here they can easy trace us."

"That's so," was the response in the voice of Jukes Dade. "Come on, boys, we'll get her out of this confounded slough if we can, and get back to town."

The voices died away as they retreated, splashing like water animals through the mud and ooze.

As silence fell once more Roy straightened up from his unpleasant situation and looked about him. The night was starry, and above his head he could see The Dipper. He knew that the outside stars of this constellation pointed to the North Star and he soon had the latter located. This gave him the points of the compass, and figuring that Acatonick must lie to the east of his present position, he struck out in that direction as nearly as he could.

He had no idea of the time, to his great chagrin, for in his haste to obey the forged summons to the flying track he had forgotten to bring his watch. In fact, in his hurry, he had slipped into an old coat, the pockets of which contained nothing more useful to him than a packet of chewing gum. He slipped a wad of this into his mouth to "keep him company" as he expressed it to himself, and grittily went forward.

The wood ended presently, and he found himself in a field with woods on all three sides, except that on which the swamp impinged. Little as he liked the idea of plunging into pathless woods, with nothing to guide him but the stars, as he glimpsed them through the trees, there was no help for it. Go on he must. Crossing the field rapidly he soon reached the border of the tangle and entered its black shadows. Keeping as straight a line as he could he hastened forward, and to his great delight, soon saw that the trees were beginning to thin out, and that beyond lay, apparently, open country.

"Hooray, I'm bound to strike a road before long now," thought Roy gleefully and quickened his pace.

He had not gone more than a few paces, however, when through the trees he heard a strange sound. It was a clinking sound like the rattling of a chain.

The boy was bold enough, but the mysterious sound on the edge of that dark wood caused his pulses to beat a bit quicker. What could it be?

Gradually, as he stood still among the trees, the sound drew closer.

"Ghosts in story books always clank chains," thought Roy, to himself. "Now if I believed in such things, I—"

He stopped short abruptly, as, from behind a clump of brush in the direction from whence the clanking had proceeded, there suddenly emerged a tall form all in white.

"Good gracious!" cried Roy, considerably startled by the sight of this sudden apparition. "I do believe—"

But at the sight of the white form he had involuntarily given a backward step. Without the slightest warning he felt the ground suddenly give way under his feet, and his body shot down through space.

Down, down he shot, a hundred mad thoughts twisting dizzily in his head.

All at once his progress was arrested. Before he could realize what had happened he felt a flood of icy cold water close over his head and a mighty ringing and roaring in his ears.

But Roy was used to diving, and he automatically, almost, held his breath till he shot to the surface again. Then he extended his hands and found that his fingers encountered a rough stone wall of some kind.

"I'm in an old well," gasped the boy as the truth suddenly flashed across him. He looked upward. Far above him, as if seen through a telescope, he could see the glittering stars. They were reflected, also, in the agitated water about him.

Somewhat to his astonishment, for the thought of death itself had been in his mind as he hurtled downward, Roy found that he was unhurt. But his present position was by no means one to invite congratulations. At the bottom of an old well in the midst of lonely fields he might stay a long time before rescue would arrive.

And in the meantime,—but Roy bravely put such thoughts resolutely out of his head, and began to feel about him to see if it was not possible to find some rough places in the sides of the excavation by which he might clamber to the surface. But his fingers only encountered stonework set far too smoothly to be of any service to him.

Then he suddenly noticed what he had not observed before, and that was that a rope depended from above, trailing its end down into the water. It was too thin to bear his weight, but the boy thought he could utilize it to keep himself above the surface without effort.

Tying a loop knot in it he thrust an arm through the noose and found that he could sustain himself very comfortably. Then he began to shout. Loudly at first—and then more feebly as his voice grew tired. But no answering sound came back to him.

For the first time since he had found himself in his predicament cold fear clutched at the young aviator's heart.

What if nobody heard him and he was compelled to remain at the bottom of the old well?

As this thought shot through his mind Roy noticed, too, that a deadly chill was beginning to creep up his limbs. He shivered waist deep in the chilly water as if he had an ague.

CHAPTER XVII.
A COWARD AND HIS WAYS.

Peggy awoke the next day with a feeling of distinct uneasiness. She and her aunt had sat up till after midnight awaiting Roy's return, but, as we know, the lad was in a position from which he could not extricate himself. An attempt had been made to communicate with the aviation grounds, but an unlucky aeroplane had blundered against the telephone wire during an afternoon flight, snapping the thread of communication.

In spite of the late hour at which they had retired, however, Miss Prescott and her niece were up betimes. But early as it was they found the little town all astir. Excursion trains were already pouring their crowds into the place and the streets were fairly alive with humanity. Peggy's first act on awaking was to gaze out of the window, beneath which some fine trees grew. Not a breath of wind stirred their leaves. The air was as clear and undisturbed as it was possible for it to be.

Donning a white duck skirt and a plain shirt waist, and dressing her hair in a becomingly simple style, Peggy hastened to the office of the hotel, and going to the telephone switchboard asked the operator to put her in communication with Roy's room. But after several minutes spent in a vain attempt to obtain an answer Central had to inform the anxious girl that there was no reply.

Thinking that after his late absence of the night before Roy might have overslept, Peggy despatched a bellboy to his room. But the report came back that the room was empty and that Roy's bed had not been slept in.

"See if you can get the executive office on the aviation grounds," said Peggy to the 'phone girl. But although the wire had been repaired and communication was easily established, there was no news of Roy. Worse still for Peggy's peace of mind, she learned now, for the first time, that there had been no meeting at the aviation field the night before.

"If your brother got a note to that effect it was a forgery," said the official who answered the call.

Peggy fairly flew upstairs to her aunt's room. Rapidly she informed Miss Prescott of what had happened.

"Oh, I'm certain now that that hateful Fanning Harding has something to do with it," she almost sobbed.

"Hush, dear," said her aunt, although in the gentle lady's breast a great fear had arisen, "everything may be all right. At any rate, I do not believe that any one, no matter how anxious they were that you should not compete in the race, would dare to resort to such methods to keep Roy out of the contest."

"I don't know so much about that, auntie," rejoined the girl. "I was in our hangar yesterday afternoon and I noticed a horrid looking man prowling about with Fanning Harding. If it had not been too improbable I should say that I knew the man's face."

"My dear!" exclaimed the good lady in astonishment.

"Well," rejoined Peggy with conviction, "I'm almost sure that the man was Jukes Dade, a workman who once was employed in his laboratory and workshop by my father. He was a skillful mechanic, but dad had to discharge him because he drank fearfully. He swore at the time that he would get even with us in some way. But we never heard any more of him. Yet if that really was him with Fanning Harding yesterday I'm awfully afraid that there is some mischief stirring."

"What you say, my dear, makes me also very anxious," responded Miss Prescott. "Perhaps we had better communicate with the police at once."

"Not yet, aunt," breathed Peggy; "you see, Roy may turn up in time for the race, and if he does, everything will be all right."

"But, Peggy—"

"On the other hand, if we spread an alarm that he is missing we shall be declared out of the contest."

"I see what you mean, my dear," was the response, "and I suppose that what you say is best. I feel positive, somehow, that we shall have news of Roy before long, and that no harm has come to him."

But the morning wore on, and no word came. In the meantime, every available source of information had been canvassed thoroughly without result. Roy Prescott had totally vanished; or so it seemed.

Peggy, as in duty bound, spent all she could spare of the morning at the aviation field, putting the finishing touches on the Golden Butterfly. The big contest was not to be held till the afternoon, and in the meantime, some of the smaller events were flown off. But Peggy was too heartsick to watch the aeroplanes thunder around the course, which was marked out by red and white "pylons" or signal towers.

Instead, she remained in the hangar and kept a watchful eye on Fanning Harding, who, with some mechanics and the same man she had noticed about the hangar the day before, was very busy over his machine, apparently. But no one obtained even a glimpse of Fanning's air craft, for it was not wheeled out, and, except when one or the other of his party dodged in or out, the doors of his hangar were closed.

In the course of the morning Fanning's father arrived, and not long after, to Peggy's unbounded delight, Jess and Jimsy and a party of friends drove up to the Prescott hangar.

"Why, Peggy, what is the matter with you? You look positively—er—er—dowdy!" exclaimed Jess, gazing at her friend after first greetings were over.

"And Roy, where is Roy?" demanded Jimsy.

"Yes, where is he? We want him to explain the points of this gasolene turkey-buzzard to us," cried Ed. Taylor, one of the gay party.

"I expect him here any minute," rejoined Peggy, and then drawing Jess and Jimsy aside she related to them, in a voice that shook in spite of herself, the mysterious occurrences of the night, and Roy's total disappearance.

"I'm going right over now and ask Fanning if he knows anything about it," announced Jimsy indignantly as soon as the girl had concluded.

"Oh, don't, please don't," begged his sister.

"I don't think it would be wise to, now," put in Peggy.

But Jimsy was not to be shaken in his purpose. Fanning was outside his hangar smoking a cigarette and swaggering about when Jimsy approached him. Perhaps the self-assertive youth felt a bit alarmed at the look in Jimsy's eye as he stepped up, but he assumed an impudent expression and blew out a puff of smoke which he did not try to avert from Jimsy's face.

"Good morning, Fanning," said Jimsy, bottling up his temper at the other's insulting manners, "can you give me a few minutes of private conversation?"

"Hum, well I don't know. What's it about?" inquired Harding more impudently than ever.

"It's about Roy, Fanning," said Jimsy seriously. "I want you to tell me on your word of honor that you don't know where he is."

"Oh, you do, eh? Well, you have an awful nerve to come to me with such questions. How do I know where he is?"

This question was somewhat of a poser for Jimsy. That impetuous youth had approached the other more or less on an impulse, and now that the direct question was put to him he felt that he could not, for the life of him, put his suspicions into so many words.

"Well—er—you see," he said somewhat confusedly, "I had an idea that you might have seen him."

"Well, I haven't, and what's more I don't want to," snapped Fanning aggressively. He was quite cool now that he saw that Jimsy had nothing definite against him in his mind, but only a vague suspicion.

"You really mean that, Fanning?" rejoined Jimsy earnestly. "His sister is terribly worried. He hasn't been seen since last night."

"Is that so?" asked Fanning with a sudden accession of interest; "then he can't race to-day, can he?"

"I wasn't thinking about the race," said Jimsy; "it was Roy himself I was worrying about."

"Well, you may as well stop your anxiety," chuckled Fanning; "how do you know he isn't off on a little spree, and—"

"That's enough, Fanning. Roy Prescott does not do such low-down things. He—"

"Oh, you mean to imply that I do, eh?"

Fanning came forward pugnaciously.

"I'll tell you what it is, Jim Bancroft, you just take yourself away from this hangar as quickly as possible. I don't want anything to do with you, do you understand? It's none of my business if Roy goes off and forgets to tell you where to find him. How do you know he hasn't gone off with those jewels?"

"What do you mean?"

Jimsy's tone was as angry in reality now as Fanning Harding's had been for effect a few seconds before.

But Fanning, in his bitter enmity toward Roy, could not see the danger signals in Jimsy's honest gray eyes.

"What do I mean?" he drawled; "why, just this, that the investigation of the police has taken a new turn in the last few days, and that Roy is likely to be arrested within the next twenty-four hours for robbery. I'll bet he got wind of it and skipped out. I'll bet—"

"How dare you?"

Peggy, eyes aflame, stepped up. Her bosom heaved angrily.

"How dare you say such things? You—you coward."

"Well, I ain't coward enough to steal a girl's jewels and then—"

"Hold on there, Fanning. Stop right there."

It was Jimsy's turn. But Fanning was too much worked up in his vindictive anger to stop.

"I won't stop," he shouted. "I'll say it right out. Roy Prescott is a—"

But before he could utter another word Jimsy's fist had shot out, and Fanning's chin happening to be in the way he felt himself suddenly propelled off his feet and elevated into the air. He sought to recover his balance as he reeled, but his foot caught in a bit of turf, and whirling his arms about like one of those figures on the top of a barn he measured his length.

"Had enough?" asked Jimsy mildly, rolling up his sleeves.

"No, you despicable young whelp!" roared Fanning, utterly throwing aside all prudence. "I haven't."

He leaped to his feet and rushed toward Jimsy. As he did so Jess gave a shriek. In the angry, half-crazed youth's hand there glistened a long clasp knife.

"Jimsy! Look out!" cried the girl.

But before the frenzied Fan could spring upon Jimsy, who was utterly unprepared for the production of the deadly weapon, a dainty foot in white canvas outing shoes and silk stockings flashed out from under Peggy's skirt. It caught Fanning as he sprang, and the next instant, for the second time that day, he fell sprawling on the ground.

CHAPTER XVIII.
THE DARING OF PEGGY.

By the time he had risen to his feet several of the officials of the track were seen approaching, and Fanning, with a scowl of deep disgust at our party, who paid little attention to him, shuffled off. At first Peggy thought that the officials had seen something of the trouble and would be angry. But it turned out that they were only coming to announce a few minor changes in the rules governing the race, and to distribute printed copies of the same.

As they passed on one of them turned and remarked casually:

"By the way, as the wind is so light we have decided to have the big contest an hour earlier than was announced, and eliminate the girls' contest, so that everybody can get home from the grounds in good time for dinner."

He hastened on to join his companions on their journey down the line of hangars, outside of which aeroplanes were sputtering and smoking, and excited aviators and mechanics hustling about.

All at once a big biplane was wheeled out and soared into the air. It carried a blue and gold streamer.

"That's Steiner of the Agassiz High School in New York City," explained Jimsy; "he's confident of winning the big prize."

Peggy made some reply. She didn't know just what. Her mind was throbbing with the idea that Roy's inexplicable absence meant that harm had come to him, and that even if he were safe the advancing of the hour of the race would put them out of it if he did not make haste.

"Look, there goes Banker of the Philadelphia Polytechnic, and Rayburn of the Boston Tech," cried Jimsy the next instant as a biplane and a graceful white-winged monoplane shot aloft on trial trips, their motors exploding loudly and a tail of blue smoke streaming out behind them. A slight cheer came from the grand stands, which were already beginning to fill, as the boy aviators shot upward.

"Oh, Roy! Roy, where are you?" sighed Peggy to herself, as she watched the young aspirants for aerial honors swinging around the course.

"I'm going over to the stand and 'phone to the police station," said Jimsy presently; "they may have news of him over there by this time."

"Oh, yes, please do," cried Peggy, as Jimsy hastened off.

When he had gone the two girls turned troubled countenances to each other.

"You poor honey," cried Jess, "I know how you are suffering. But don't worry, Peggy, I'm sure it will come out all right."

"Yes, but—but you don't know what depends on Roy's winning this race," cried Peggy. "I am sure that some of our rivals in the race—I need not mention who—have something to do with his disappearance."

"What do you mean by saying 'a lot depends on it,' girlie?" asked Jess, drawing Peggy's arm within her own.

With brimming eyes Peggy told her friend frankly and fully what she had not before, namely, the exact circumstances of the Prescott family and the threat which old Harding held above their heads.

"So, you see, Jess," she concluded sadly, "this could not have happened at a worse time for us."

"I see that," gently rejoined the other girl, "but listen, dear, you may have a chance to win it after all if you will trust to us to find Roy."

"Trust to you?" repeated Peggy in a puzzled tone. "Trust to you to find Roy?"

"Yes, my dear, while you—go in and win the race!"

"Why, what are you talking about?" gasped Peggy.

"A brilliant idea that has just occurred to me. You are about Roy's height, and if your hair was cut short you'd look enough like him to be his twin brother instead of his sister. But that doesn't matter, for you wear goggles and a helmet in driving that thing, anyway, don't you?"

"Yes. But,—oh, Jess, I couldn't do that."

"Not even for your aunt's sake, Peggy, and to show those whom you suspect that they could not put a Prescott out of the race, however hard they tried? Come into the shed with me. I am going to persuade you, if I can, to do a brave thing."

With their arms about each other's waists the girls walked toward the hangar and entered it. As they did so the figure of Jukes Dade glided from a place of concealment close at hand, and slipping behind some low bushes he gained the rear of the Prescott shed unperceived. Once there he placed an ear to a crack in the structure, from within which could be heard the murmur of girlish voices.

Whatever he heard seemed to strike him with astonishment at first and then with a malicious glee.

"So," he muttered, "that's your scheme, is it? Well, I guess we'll be able to head that off. That aeroplane of yours won't go in that race if I can help it, and even if it did I know enough now to head you off from getting the big prize. That young Harding ought to pay me well for this."

So saying, Jukes Dade shuffled off toward Fanning's hangar, still chortling evilly to himself.

Jimsy returned to the shed without any good news. In fact, the doleful expression on his usually merry face would have told them that long before he opened his mouth. In the midst of the general gloom a merry face was suddenly obtruded through the swinging doors.

"Hullo! hullo! young folks, what's the trouble? You look as if you were going to attend a funeral."

They looked up to see the figure of Hal Homer, clad in white flannels, and with a checked cap on his curly head, standing in the doorway.

"Can I come in?" he asked, and without waiting for an answer in he came.

"Oh, Mr. Homer," cried Jess, fairly pouncing on him, "we're so glad you've come; we are in a dreadful fix."

"A dreadful fix? Why, my dear young lady, I read in the local paper that I bought on my way from the depot that Roy's machine, judging from the trials, was going to have things all her own way."

"So much so," struck in Jimsy, "that it looks as if some of Roy's enemies have spirited him away."

"What? I'm afraid I hardly understand."

The aviation instructor looked at Jimsy in a puzzled way, rather as if he thought the youth might be having some fun with him.

"No, no, this is serious. I mean it," spoke Jimsy quickly. "Roy has gone!"

"Gone!"

"Yes. He vanished last night. But sit down and we'll tell you all about it. Maybe you can help us out."

Absolutely "flabbergasted," to use his own expression, the good-looking young flying man sank down on an upturned case, while Jimsy went on to relate all that had occurred, with Peggy every now and then striking in with additions and corrections.

Another ear also took in the conversation—that of Jukes Dade—who had seen the arrival of the well-dressed young aviator, and had instantly slipped back to his eavesdropping post to learn what the newcomer's business might be.

It might have been an hour later that a chauffeur, summoned by 'phone from the grandstand, brought the Bancrofts' car up to the hangar and Hal Homer, Jess and Jimsy emerged.

"Drive to the police station," ordered Hal Homer as he stepped in, leaving Jess and Jimsy behind.

Jukes Dade, peering around a corner of the hangar, heard the order and grew pale.

"Looks bad," he muttered as the car rolled off; "I wonder if they know anything. If they do, I'm off. This isn't a healthy part of the country for Jukes Dade from the minute that kid is found. He didn't recognize Gid or young Harding, but he knew me all right. I could tell it by the way he looked at me, and if he's found the first man they'll hunt for is me."

With snake-like caution he glided behind the hangar once more.

It was not long after this that the Golden Butterfly was wheeled out by some of the mechanicians attached to the track, whose services were furnished free by the aviation officials.

Jess and Jimsy emerged from the hangar at the same time, in company with a boyish figure in aviator's clothing, leather trousers cut very baggily, fur-lined leather coat and big helmet of leather, well padded, completely obscuring the features. After a few words in a low tone with its companions, this figure clambered lightly into the aeroplane, leaned forward, adjusted some levers, and the next instant, amidst a shout from several hastily gathered onlookers, the Golden Butterfly skyrocketed upward, her engine roaring like an angry giant hornet.

All this was watched by Fanning Harding, Jukes Dade, and Gid Gibbons.

"A nice mess you've made of it," growled Harding angrily to his companions. "You've succeeded in getting me suspected, and in trouble, while the boy is safe and sound and on the scene."

"Wonder how he got back," grunted Gid speculatively; "he must have looked a sight when he crawled out of that swamp."

"Say, Dade, you'd better be off," said Fanning suddenly; "you were the only one of us whose face wasn't covered. He would swear to you."

"Oh, I ain't worrying yet," grinned Dade easily.

"You're not, eh? Well, you are a cool hand," rejoined Gid admiringly. "If I were in your shoes I'd clear out before that aeroplane lands again."

"You would, eh?" scoffed Dade. "Well, what would you say if I told you that that ain't Roy Prescott in the Golden Butterfly at all?"

"That you were crazy with the heat," was the prompt and impolite answer.

"Then you'd be crazy yourself. That's his sister in that aeroplane, and if he don't show up in time for the race she's going to fly it herself and win it."

If a bombshell had fallen at Fanning's feet he could not have been more thunderstruck. But he recovered in an instant.

"If she does I'll protest to the judges," he said angrily; "they can't prove that I know anything about her brother's disappearance, and that Golden Butterfly won't win this race if I can help it."

CHAPTER XIX.
BROTHER AND SISTER.

The first gleam of the summer dawn shining into Roy's place of imprisonment at the bottom of the old well revealed to him only too clearly into what a trap he had fallen. The well seemed to be about fifty feet or more in depth, and the sides were smooth and slippery.

The chill he had felt spreading through his limbs earlier was gone now, but a numb sensation was setting in which did not leave them even when the boy wriggled his legs about.

"Phew!" thought Roy. "I stand a fair chance of being turned into a pollywog or something if I stay here long enough."

Somehow, with the coming of daylight, the buoyant spirits of youth had returned to the boy and his predicament did not seem nearly so serious as it had during the dark hours.

But it was bad enough, as Roy realized. From time to time he tried shouting, but no one came to the edge of the well and peered over, although he anxiously kept his eyes riveted on the disc of sky above him. How long this went on Roy had no idea, but he had sunk into a sort of semi-doze when a sudden sound aroused him.

A tinkling, metallic sound, not unlike the rattling of the chain the night before that had, in reality, caused his trouble.

"Help! Help!" shouted Roy.

It was perhaps the five hundredth time he had uttered the cry since he had tumbled into the well. But this time there came a response.

"What is it? What's the trouble?"

The voice sounded rather shaky, and as if the utterer of the words was somewhat scared.

"It's a boy who has fallen into the well," shouted Roy. "I'm almost exhausted. Get me out."

A face suddenly projected over the well curb—a face which Roy recognized with astonishment as that of old Peter Bell, the hermit.

"Mr. Bell, it's Roy Prescott," he shouted; "can you get a rope and get me out?"

"Good heavens!" cried the hermit; "it's the boy whose sister was so kind to me. However did you—but never mind that now. Can you hold on for a time?"

"Yes, but my strength is almost gone."

"Well, summon up all your courage. There is a farm house not far off. I'll go there and get a rope and be back as quick as I can."

Without wasting more words the old man hastened to his little cart. He had been out since dawn gathering herbs and roots and had taken a short cut home through the field in which the old well was located. Muttering excitedly to himself, he climbed somewhat stiffly into his rickety conveyance and urged his old horse forward with gently spoken commands. As the animal broke into a trot the little bell about its neck began to jangle not unmusically. This was the sound which, fortunately for him, had notified Roy that some human being was at hand.

In the near distance, half hidden in trees, could be seen the red-roofed gable of a farm house. Toward this old Peter Bell directed his way. Farmer Ingalls was only too glad, when he heard of the accident, to secure a long rope, used in hoisting hay to the top of his big barns.

"Bless my soul!" he exclaimed, "a lad tumbled into my well! Mommer," turning to a motherly-looking, calico-clad woman, "you always told me to cover that well up, and I never did, and now thar's a poor young chap tumbled into it."

"Hurry," urged old Peter Bell; "he was almost exhausted, poor lad. We must get back as quick as possible."

Summoning his two hired men the farmer set off at a run across the fields, easily keeping pace with old Peter's decrepit horse. As they neared the well they began shouting, and a feeble cry from the depths answered them.

"Cheer up, my lad, we'll have you out of that in a brace-of-shakes," cried Farmer Ingalls encouragingly, as they reached the curb and peered over into the dark hole.

"I hope you will," cried Roy. "It's getting pretty monotonous, I can tell you."

"Don't know what mon-ount-on-tonous means, but I'd hate to change places with you," agreed the farmer.

Presently the rope came snaking down, with a loop in its lower end. Roy was directed to place his foot in the loop and hold on tight. When this had been done he shouted up:

"All right! Haul away!"

The stalwart farmer and his two assistants began to heave with all their might, while old Mr. Bell encouraged them. Before long, by dint of hard exertions, they succeeded in dragging Roy to the surface, and dripping and shivering he could stand once more in the blessed air and sunlight.

"But how in the world did you come to get in there?" asked the farmer, as he paced along by the side of the hermit's little cart, in which the half-exhausted Roy had been placed.

"Well," said the lad with a rather shamefaced laugh, "I'm really half ashamed to say. But it was this way. Some bad men who have an interest in putting me out of an aeroplane contest, of which Mr. Bell knows, had run off with me in an automobile. It was wrecked, and I escaped. I struck out toward town, as I thought, but as I came through that patch of woods by the wall I saw something that startled me so much that I stepped back and fell down the well."

"What did you see, my lad?" asked the farmer with half a twinkle in his eye.

"Something like a story-book ghost," smiled Roy; "it was tall and all in white and clanked a chain."

"Ha! ha! ha!" roared the farmer; "I half suspected as much. Why, that ghost was my old white mule Boxer. He managed somehow to snap his chain last night and we found him careening around the fields this morning. Don't color up, my boy," for poor Roy's face had turned very red, as the hired men guffawed loudly; "older men than you have been startled at far less. And now, here's the farm, and I'll bet mommer has a fine breakfast all ready for you."

The half-famished boy ate hungrily of the substantial farmhouse fare Mrs. Ingalls provided for him, and as he ate he made inquiries about the distance to the aviation grounds, which, he found to his dismay, were further distant than he had imagined.

"I'll never be able to make it in time without an automobile," moaned Roy to himself; "what shall I do?"

He cast about in his mind for some way out of his difficulty, but he could find none. Nor could the farmer help him. There were no automobiles in that part of the country, and in a horse-drawn vehicle he would never be able to make it in time.

All at once a queer sound filled the air. The atmosphere seemed to vibrate with it as it does on a still summer day when a threshing machine is buzzing away in a distant field.

"Land o' Goshen, what's that?" cried Mrs. Ingalls running to the door.

"Lish! Lish! come here quick!" she shouted the next instant.

Followed by the old hermit and Roy, Mr. Ingalls ran to the door. But his exclamations at the sight he saw were drowned by Roy's amazed cry:

"It's the Golden Butterfly!"

"An aeroplane!" shouted the farmer. "By gosh, she's like a pretty bird."

"It's my—our aeroplane," went on Roy; "who can be in it? Oh, if it's only Peggy I may not be too late after all."

He ran out into the door yard of the farm house and, snatching off his coat, began waving it desperately. Would the occupant of the aeroplane see his frantic signals? With a beating heart Roy watched the winged machine as it droned far above him.

All at once he gave a delighted shout. The aeroplane was beginning to descend. Down it came in big circles, while the farmer, his wife and the old hermit gazed open mouthed at it, as if half inclined to run.

But as it drew closer to the ground Roy noted a puzzling thing. A helmeted and goggled person was driving it, evidently a boy or man and not Peggy at all. Who could it be? For an instant a queer thought flashed through his head. Possibly somebody had stolen it and was making off across country with it so as to put it out of the race.

More and more rapidly the aeroplane began to drop as it neared the ground, and before many minutes it alighted in the patch of meadow in front of the farm house, gliding gracefully for several feet before it stopped.

But the rubber-tired landing wheels had not ceased revolving before Roy was at its side.

"Say, who are you, and what are you doing with my aeroplane?" he demanded in heated tones, for the helmeted aviator had not yet even deigned to notice him, but seemed to be busy with various levers and valves.

"Well, are you going to answer me?" sputtered Roy, while the farmer, his wife, the old hermit and the hired men gazed on curiously.

For answer the mysterious aviator raised his helmet and a cloud of golden curls fell about a milk-and-roses face.

"By gum, a gal and a purty one!" cried the farmer capering about.

"Peggy!" shouted Roy.

"Yes, Peggy," cried the girl. "Oh, Roy, what has happened to you? When you didn't come back Jess and Jimsy persuaded me to put on your clothes and at least try the Butterfly out. But I was so miserable that I could not try her out on the track, so I flew off across country. I saw you waving far below me and—oh, Roy!"

Peggy could go no further and half collapsed in Roy's arms as he tenderly lifted her out.

"Great hopping water millions!" cried the farmer, "if this ain't a day of wonders. This must be ther lad's sister he told us about, and ter think she come flopping down out of ther sky like a seventeen-y'ar locust."

Peggy was quickly her usual strong, self-reliant self again. With indignation blazing in her kind eyes she heard Roy's account of the happenings of the night. At its conclusion she announced with decision:

"We must defeat them, Roy."

"Yes, but how? There's only a scant half hour before starting time if you said they'd changed it."

"Even so you can make it. You must take these clothes, get into the aeroplane and fly back to the track. If you go alone the 'plane will be light and you can make it in time."

"But you, Peggy?"

"I guess I can borrow a dress from Mrs. Ingalls here," said the girl briskly.

"Of course, you kin," put in Mrs. Ingalls, but surveying her own ample form rather doubtfully the while.

"You kin give her one of daughter Jenny's dresses," said the farmer.

"Then that is settled, thanks to you," said Peggy with characteristic decision.

They all entered the farm house, from which, a few seconds later, Roy emerged, clad in the garments his sister had donned a short time before. He climbed into the aeroplane amid the admiring comments of the farm hands, who, by this time, had come in from the fields, drawn by the wonderful airship, and stood all about it gaping and wondering.

Peggy, in a dress belonging to the farmer's daughter, who was away on a visit, stepped quickly to Roy's side as, after glancing at the clock attached to the front of the aeroplane, he started the engine.

As it started its uproarious song, the farm hands jumped back in affright. But Peggy clasped her brother's hand.

"Win that prize, Roy," she said.

"I'll do my best, little sister."

And that was all, but as Peggy Prescott gazed a few minutes later at the fast diminishing form of the speeding aeroplane she felt that all she had braved and dared that day had not been in vain.

CHAPTER XX.
IN THE NICK OF TIME.

Excitement had reached its topmost pitch on the aviation field. It was but a few minutes to starting time for the great contest, and already four young aviators had their winged craft in line before the judge's stand.

Engines were belching clouds of acrid blue smoke heavily impregnated with oily, smelling fumes. The roar of motors shook the air. Folks in the grandstand and on the crowded lawns excitedly pointed out to one another the different machines, all of which bore large numbers.

Excited officials, red-faced and perspiring, bustled about importantly, while from the top of the judge's stand a portly man bellowed occasional announcements through a megaphone.

Suddenly he made an announcement that caused a hum of interest.

"Machine number seven—mach-ine num-ber sev-en! Fanning Harding, owner, has withdrawn from the race," he announced.

A buzz of comment went through the crowd. Jess, Jimsy and Hal Homer, standing in a group by the empty Prescott hangar, exchanged astonished glances as they heard the news. What did that mean? Fanning had been swaggering about, boasting of his wonderful aeroplane, and now it appeared at the eleventh hour he had decided not to enter it.

"Must have had an accident," opined Jimsy.

"Maybe he gave it one of those pleasant looks of his," suggested Jess.

"Wherever can Peggy be," exclaimed the girl the next minute; "she's been gone for more than an hour. I do hope nothing has happened to her."

"Not likely," rejoined Jimsy, although he looked a little troubled over the non-appearance of the Golden Butterfly.

"The police said they had a dragnet out in every part of the vicinity," volunteered Hal Homer, who had returned only a few minutes before from the station house.

Bang!

A bomb had been shot skyward and now exploded in a cloud of yellow smoke.

"Three minutes to starting time," cried Hal Homer anxiously; "where can Miss Prescott be?"

"Look!" cried Jess suddenly, dancing about. "Oh, Glory! Here she comes!"

Far off against the sky a speck was visible. Rushing toward them at tremendous speed it swiftly grew larger. The crowd saw it now and great excitement prevailed. The word flew about that the machine was the missing Number Six. Would it arrive in time to participate in the start and thus qualify? This was the question on every lip.

Hal Homer jumped into the auto and sped over to the judge's stand.

"Can't you delay the start for five minutes?" he begged.

"Impossible," was the reply.

"But that aeroplane, Number Six, has been delayed by some accident. If you start the race on time it may not arrive in time to take part."

"Can't be helped. Young Prescott—that's the name of the owner, isn't it?—shouldn't have gone off on a cross country tryout."

Back to the hangar sped Hal, where Jess and Jimsy, almost beside themselves with excitement, were watching the homing aeroplane.

"She'll be on time," cried Jimsy as the graceful ship swept over the distant confines of the course and came thundering down toward the starting point.

A great cheer swept skywards as the aeroplane came on.

"She'll make it."

"She won't."

"Where has the thing been?"

"Why is it so late?"

These and a hundred other questions and remarks went from mouth to mouth all through the big crowd.

"It's all off," groaned Jimsy suddenly.

He had seen the signal corps man, whose duty it was to fire the bombs, outstretching himself on the ground awaiting the signal to touch off the starting sign.

But even as Jimsy spoke, the Golden Butterfly made a swift turn and, amid a roar from the crowd, shot whirring past the grandstand and alighted in front of the stand on the starting line.

Hardly had the wheels touched the ground before the judge in charge of the track raised his hand. A flag fell and the signal corps man jerked his arm back, firing the bomb that announced the start.

B-o-o-o-o-m!

As the detonation died out the aeroplanes shot forward, rising into the still air almost in a body, like a flock of birds. It was a spectacle never to be forgotten, and the crowd appreciated it to the full.

But up in the grandstand, in inconspicuous places, sat three persons who did not look as well pleased as those about them.

"So the girl is going to take a chance," muttered Fanning Harding; "well, so much the worse for her. If she wins I'll put in a protest and compel her to unmask."

"Won't that Prescott and Bancroft bunch be astonished when they find out that we are on to their little game," chuckled Jukes Dade; "it'll be as good as a play."

"That's what it will," grinned Gid.

"They'll find out that they can't humiliate me and not suffer for it," grated out Fanning.

"Wonder where that girl went to on her tryout spin?" inquired Dade.

"It doesn't make much difference where, but she certainly came back with a grandstand play," rejoined Gid.

"Well, if she wins the race it will be our turn," Fanning assured him.

They then turned their attention to the contest, two laps of which had been made while they were talking.

Number One, a small white Bleriot type of monoplane, seemed to be making the pace for the rest, and word flew about that it had gained half a lap on Number Four, its nearest competitor so far.

"But it will be a long contest," said the wiseacres in the crowd, "and accidents may happen at any time."

On the fourth lap Number One was seen to descend over by the hangars. Something had gone wrong with its lubricating valve. By the time the difficulty was adjusted it was hopelessly out of the race. Number Three was the next to drop out. This machine was driven by one of the high school lads, and his contingent of rooters in the grandstand set up a woeful noise as he dropped to earth in the middle of the course. A broken stay had made it dangerous for him to remain longer in the air.

This left number Six, the Prescott machine, Numbers Two, Four and Five still in the air.

"Number Six has gained a lap on Number Five!" went up the cry presently as Number Five, so far the leader, was seen to lose speed on the fifteenth lap.

The Golden Butterfly was in truth doing magnificently, but try as her operator would it did not seem possible to shake off Number Five, another high school boy's machine, which clung persistently to its stern. Number Four alighted for more gasolene on the twentieth lap and lost a round of the course thereby. A few seconds later Number Two was also forced to descend with heated cylinders. This practically left the race between Number Five and the Golden Butterfly. Round and round they tore, neither of them gaining or losing a foot apparently. The thunder of their engines grew deafeningly monotonous and the crowds watched them as if hypnotized by the whirring aerial monsters.

All at once, though, a mighty roar proclaimed that something was happening, and gazing down toward the further end of the track it could be seen that Number Six, the Golden Butterfly, had made a daring attempt to gain on the other machine, and had succeeded.

So close did the two aeroplanes edge to the end pylon in the effort to secure the inside plane that for an instant it looked as if a crash must result.

A thunder of cheers greeted the Golden Butterfly as she swept by the grandstand on the next lap.

"That girl can drive all right," grudgingly admitted Fanning Harding.

"Yes, and she's pretty as a picture, too," put in Gid Gibbons; "guess you were stuck on her once, weren't you, Fan?"

"Oh, shut up," growled Fanning angrily. "It makes no difference to you, does it?"

The aeroplanes had been racing for an hour now, and neither showed any signs of slacking speed. On the contrary, as they "warmed up," they seemed to go the quicker. All at once an incident occurred which brought the crowd to its feet yelling and cheering as if wild.

The driver of Number Five, as the two machines passed the grandstand, had made a deliberate attempt to prevent the Golden Butterfly overhauling him by jamming his aeroplane over toward a pylon and directly in front of the Butterfly. For an instant it looked as if a crash must be inevitable, but just as the spectators were beginning to turn pale and the more timid to hide their eyes, the Butterfly was seen to make a graceful dip and dive clean under the other aeroplane. It was a magnificent bit of aerial driving, and the crowd appreciated it to the full. A roar and a shout went up, to which the driver of Number Six responded with a wave of a gloved hand.

Ten minutes later Number Five, two laps behind, and with a leaking radiator, dropped out of the race, leaving the Golden Butterfly the winner. Fanning Harding was white as a sheet as he saw an official with a black and white checkered flag step out into the field. This was the signal to the Golden Butterfly, which was still in the air, that the race was over.

As the Prescott aeroplane dropped to earth in front of the grandstand amid rapturous plaudits, the son of the Sandy Bay banker deliberately arose and made his way toward the judges' stand, to which Hal Homer and the Bancrofts, the core of a shouting, yelling mob of enthusiasts, were already conducting the daring driver of Number Six.

Special policemen made a path for the aviator and his friends, while cries of:

"Take off your helmet!"

"We want to see you!"

"What's the matter with Number Six?" and a hundred other cries arose.

But the driver of Number Six did not respond, and with his helmet still on his head was conducted before the judges to receive their congratulations. The helmet was still in place when Fanning Harding came shoving through the crowd and finally reached the little group.

"As a competitor I demand that Number Six take off his helmet!" he cried.

The judges turned to him in astonishment.

"This is most unseemly, sir," said one of them; "no doubt in good time Mr. Prescott will take off his helmet."

"Oh, no, he won't," shouted Fanning, at whom all the group was now gazing. "He won't, I tell you, and for a good reason, too. That's not Roy Prescott at all, but his sister Peggy."

But the words had not left his lips before Jimsy, with a quick motion, jerked off the aviator's helmet and disclosed the handsome, perspiring features of Roy himself.

In the few minutes he had had, Roy had found time briefly to explain how he and his sister had changed garments.

"Well, I guess that settles that question," cried Jimsy triumphantly, as a mighty shout went up.

"It certainly does," said one of the officials. "Where is that young scamp? Officer, find the young man who made that accusation and bring him here to explain himself."

But the disgruntled Fanning had dived off into the crowd the instant he saw into what a tremendous blunder he had fallen. And although a strict search was made for him he was not to be found.

CHAPTER XXI.
THE PHANTOM AIRSHIP.

In the midst of the hum and excitement and the crossfire of questions which immediately followed, there occurred a startling interruption. From the further side of the grounds there arose a cry, which swelled in volume as it advanced.

"Fire! One of the hangars is on fire!"

The group immediately broke up and orders and commands flew thick and fast. In the midst of the excitement Roy and his chums found an opportunity to slip away.

"There's the fire. Off by our hangar!" shouted Hal Homer, pointing across the field.

By the side of the Prescott's green aero shed a big cloud of smoke was ascending, mingled with yellow flames. It seemed to be a hot blaze.

"It's Fanning Harding's hangar!" cried Roy suddenly; "come on, let's go over and see what the matter is."

"I've got the car right here," said Jimsy. "I'll get you over in a jiffy."

Soon they were speeding across the field toward the blaze. In the meantime an emergency fire corps, composed of men employed on the grounds, had attached a line of hose to a hydrant and were drenching the flames. Such good work did they do that it was not long before they had the fire under control.

As soon as it was out our party, which had managed to get through the lines formed to keep back the curious, gazed into the ruins with some interest.

"Why, say!" cried Jimsy suddenly, "the place was empty."

"So it was!" cried Roy in astonished tones, "except for that big box kite over in the corner there. Whatever kind of a game of bluff has Fanning Harding been playing?"

"I guess I can imagine it," struck in Hal Homer. "From what you have told me his little game was to bluff you into thinking he had a fine airship that could beat yours, and in that way induce you to sell out to him."

"By George, I never thought of that!" exclaimed Roy, "but—hullo, here comes Peggy in the farmer's wagon!"

He ran through the crowd to the side of the wagon, which had been driven in by Farmer Ingalls.

"You dear, dear boy, I've heard all about it already," cried Peggy, throwing her white arms about Roy's neck, while Miss Prescott, whom they had picked up at the hotel, sat by, hardly knowing whether to laugh or to cry, as she expressed it later.

I am not going to describe that reunion by the side of Fanning Harding's burned hangar, but each reader can imagine for herself what a joyous one it was.

"I know a place in town where they sell the bulliest sodas and sundaes," cried Jimsy suddenly. "Everybody come up there in the car and we'll celebrate!"

"In one moment, Jimsy," said Roy. "There's one thing still I don't understand about this whole business, and that is this. It is clear enough that Fanning Harding was bluffing about having an aeroplane in that shed, but how was it that he made a night ascent with red and green lanterns?"

"Oh, you mean the time you saw him in the air at night, the time we went to Washington?" asked Jimsy.

"That's it. How do you account for it?"

"Give it up," rejoined the other lad.

"Perhaps this may help to explain it."

Hal Homer came up carrying two much scorched lanterns he had found in the debris of the hangar. One was red, the other was green.

"I don't quite see," said Peggy, but Hal, with an apology interrupted her.

"It's plain as day to me," he said; "these two lanterns attached to that big box kite on a breezy night would certainly give any one the impression that an aeroplane was sailing about. Harding knew you would be flying home in that vicinity on that night and rigged up this contrivance to delude you."

"A phantom airship!" cried Peggy.

"That's about the size of it," put in the slangy Jimsy, "and I think that friend Homer here has hit on the correct solution."

"But if that were so, why did Fanning fit up a shop out at Gid Gibbons's place?" asked Jess in a puzzled tone.

"I guess that shop had no more in it than this hangar," was Roy's reply. "Gid Gibbons is a bad character who would do anything for money, and I think it likely that he fell in with Harding's schemes because he had no great liking for any of us."

"Looks that way," agreed Jimsy.

"But that doesn't explain that ruby which Hester was wearing," thought Peggy to herself as the laughing party of young folks drove off up the town, followed by Farmer Ingalls and his good wife, who had been invited to take part in the little celebration of their triumph. Here and there they were recognized and cheered, but among the crowds on the sidewalks all discussing the thrilling race, there were three that took no part in the good-natured jubilation. Who these were we can guess.

Jukes Dade at Fanning's side had to listen to some savage abuse as they slunk along, avoiding as far as possible the crowds.

"I told you to burn up the hangar so that there would be no trace left of the bluff we had been putting up," he growled.

"Well, didn't I soak the place with gasolene," protested Dade; "how was I to know a kid would come along and give the alarm before it got fairly alight?"

"It's been a dismal failure all the way through," lamented Harding, as if he had been engaged on some praiseworthy enterprise.

"Incidentally," purred Jukes Dade, but with a menace under his silky tones, "I'd like to see some of that money you've been promising me all along."

"You'll have to wait till I see my father," snapped out Fanning savagely.

"Well, see him quick then, or I may have to take other means of getting it," snarled Dade.

"What do you mean?"

"Why, by telling a few things I know. About the loss of a certain lady's jewels, for instance."

Fanning went white as ashes.

"You sneak! You've been listening at keyholes!" he cried.

Dade returned him look for look defiantly.

"Well, what if I have?" he snarled. "I've got a hold on you now, Master Harding. I've got you where I want you and I'm going to keep you there."

CHAPTER XXII.
JIM BELL OF THE WEST.

Some days after the events described in the last chapter, and following the receipt by Roy of a pink check for $5,000.00, a strange visitor arrived at the Prescott home—their very own home now, for the mortgage had been paid off, much to Mr. Harding's disgust.

The stranger was a bronzed man and wore a broad-brimmed sombrero which would have marked him anywhere as a Westerner. Of Miss Prescott, who, in a new lavender silk dress, came to the door, he inquired if he could see Mr. Roy Prescott.

Miss Prescott smiled at this ceremonial way of mentioning her young nephew, but directed the stranger with the breezy Western manner to the workshop at the rear of the house, where Roy and Peggy were "fussing," as Jess called it, with their beloved Golden Butterfly.

"Good morning," he said, doffing his sombrero with a sweep and a flourish; "can I have a word with you?"

"Certainly. Two or three if you want them," rejoined Roy, while Peggy gazed in some surprise at the queer-mannered newcomer.

"The fact is," went on the stranger, "that I'm in the market for aeroplanes such as yours. I happened to be on the train some nights ago when you came flying through the air with two belated young passengers. Well, sir, thinks I, if such a machine can make a train on schedule time it ought to be good for other purposes. I took the liberty of making some inquiries about you from your two young friends after the train had started, but asked them not to mention the matter to you yet awhile.

"In New York I looked up my partner and we discussed the plan and he agreed with me that it was a good one. Now, I'm down here this morning to offer you $10,000 outright for the use of half a dozen of your aeroplanes, and a salary of $5,000 as instructor to the aviators I shall have to have to run them. How does the offer strike you?"

"I—er—well, I hardly know what to say," responded Roy; "you see, it's a bit sudden. It rather takes my breath away."

"Well, that's a way we have in the West," was the response, "but maybe I'd better tell you a little more about myself. My name is Jim Bell. I'm worth a couple of million or thereabouts. You can verify that by referring to the First National Bank of 'Frisco, or the East Coast Bank of New York City. I've got interests in cattle, wool and mines, but the very best mining proposition I ever struck I ran across out on the Nevada alkali desert in a range of barren hills. We were prospecting there when I was told about it. After untold hardships I found the spot and staked it out. But there arose the difficulty of transportation. There was the gold all right, but how was I to get it out?"

"I came East to see if I couldn't get some sort of automobile built that would travel the desert, but when I saw that aeroplane of yours droop down at that jerkwater junction, I realized I had found what I wanted. Now, are you on?"

"You'll have to give us a little time to think, sir," rejoined Roy; "it's a very flattering offer and I'd like to accept it, but I'll have to think it over."

"Quite right, quite right," rejoined the other, "nothing like thinking it over. If every one did that fewer accidents and mishaps would occur in life. Take my own life, for instance. I've often thought I'd go back to see the old folks, but in that case I thought it over too long, for when I went to the old home the other day it was all gone. Not a stick or stone remained. My parents were dead and my only brother was no-one-knew-where."

Jim Bell's voice shook strangely. He blinked his eyes once or twice and then resumed briskly: "You see, I left home in a mighty queer way. I was out in a boat with my brother when it got overturned. He was drowned, I guess, but anyway I found myself drifting about on the Sound. I managed to seize hold of a bit of floating driftwood and in that way kept my head above water till a ship came along and picked me up.

"She was a big vessel bound for China and her captain was a brute. On our arrival in the Far East he bound me out as a sort of apprentice to a rich Chinaman living in the interior. I was with him for ten years before I escaped. I worked my way to the coast, got another ship and headed for California.

"On the way across there was a mutiny and I saved the life of a wealthy passenger, who turned out to be a mining man and who, when he died two years later, left me most of his property. That gave me my start in life, and now I'm a millionaire. But I'd give it all if I could get some news of poor brother Peter and find out if he is dead or alive."

"Maybe we can help you," cried Peggy, her eyes shining and her white hands clasped excitedly.

While the rugged Westerner had been talking the story of the old hermit came back to her.

"What do you mean?" asked the other; "do you know where my brother is?"

"I'm not certain," cried Peggy, "but the old hermit, Peter Bell, is he almost beyond a doubt."

"My brother a hermit!" cried the wealthy mining man.

"If it is your brother," put in Roy, "I hope for your sake it is. But his story tallies absolutely with yours. He told us that after he had missed you in the water he thought that you were drowned. Returning home he was shunned on every side, for the villagers accused him of having deserted you to save his own life."

"My poor Peter," breathed the miner.

"Miserable and made morose by the contempt he met with on every side he became a hermit and now lives in a hut near the town of Acatonick."

"How long does it take to get there? I must lose no time in finding out," exclaimed Jim Bell.

"You can get there in two or three hours from here if you can catch a train," said Roy. "If you like I'll phone for you and find out."

"Say, boy, that would be mighty white of you. I tell you it hurts to think of poor Peter living all alone like that in poverty while I've been rich all these years. But it wasn't for lack of trying to locate him, for I've advertised and had detectives searching every likely place."

Roy found that there would be a train to Acatonick in about half an hour, and their new found friend hastened off, after warm farewells, to catch it. He promised to be back within a few days and let them know of his success, and also inform them of any further arrangements he might be prepared to make about his offer.

"Well," said Roy, after he had gone, "the skies are beginning to clear, sis."

Peggy sighed.

"Yes, but there is still one thing to be cleared up, Roy," she said.

"I know — the disappearance of those jewels," rejoined Roy. "Oh, if only we had something more to go upon than mere suspicions."

"Perhaps we will have before long," said Peggy, musingly.

CHAPTER XXIII.
LIKE THIEVES IN THE NIGHT.

"Heard anything of Fanning Harding?" asked Jimsy, one bright morning, as he stopped his car at the Prescotts' gate and he and Jess got out.

"Not a thing since that day at Acatonick," responded Roy, who with his sister had hastened to meet the other two. "Why, Jess, how charming you look this morning."

"Meaning that you notice the contrast with other mornings," laughed Jess merrily; "oh, Roy, you are not a courtier."

"No, I guess not yet—whatever a courtier may be," was the laughing rejoinder; "but I always like to pay deserved compliments."

"Oh, that's better," cried Jess; "but have you heard anything more from Mr. Bell?"

For, of course, Jimsy and Jess by this time knew about the visit of the mining man. Mr. Bancroft had looked up his standing and character and had found both of the highest. On his advice Roy had about decided to accept the unique offer made him by the Western millionaire.

Peggy shook her head in response to Jess's question.

"No, dear, not one word," she said; "isn't it queer? However, I guess we shall, before long. Oh, I do hope that that poor old hermit turns out to be Mr. Jim Bell's brother."

"So do I, too," agreed Jimsy. "It would be jolly for you and Roy to think that you and your aeroplane had been the means of righting such a succession of mishaps."

"Indeed it would," agreed Peggy, warmly; "but now come into the house and have some ice cream. It's one sign of our new prosperity that we are never without it now."

"I've eaten so much of it I'm ashamed to look a freezer in the face," laughed Roy, as they trooped in, to be warmly welcomed by Miss Prescott.

In the midst of their merry feast the sound of wheels was heard and a rig from the station drove up. Out of it stepped a venerable old gentleman in a well-fitting dark suit, with well blackened shoes and an altogether neat and prosperous appearance.

Peggy and Jess who had run to the window at the sound of wheels saw him assisted to the ground by a younger man whom they both recognized with a cry of astonishment.

"Mr. Jim Bell. But who is the old gentleman?"

"Why it's—it's the hermit!" cried Roy.

"Good gracious, is that fashionable looking old man a hermit?" gasped Jimsy.

"He was, I guess, but he won't be any more," laughed Peggy, happily, as she tripped to the door to welcome the visitors. The Prescotts had a maid now; but Peggy preferred to be the first to greet the newly united brothers for it was evident that Jim Bell's quest had been successful.

What greetings there were to be sure, when the two brothers were inside the cool, shady house! The old hermit's eyes gleamed delightedly as he gallantly handed Miss Prescott to a chair. As for Jim Bell, he was happy enough to "dance a jig," he said.

"I'll play for you, sir," volunteered Jimsy, going toward the piano.

"No, no," laughed Jim Bell; "I'm too old for that now. But not too old for Peter and I to have many happy days together yet, eh, Peter?"

He turned tenderly toward the old man whose eyes grew dim and moist.

"I wish dad and mother could see us now," he said, sadly, as his thoughts wandered back over the long bitter years he had spent in solitude.

"Perhaps they can," breathed Peggy, softly; "let us hope so."

"Thank you," said the old hermit, with a sigh.

But the conversation soon turned to a merrier vein. And then it drifted into business. Mr. Bancroft happened to stop in on his way into town and after a long talk with Jim Bell he seriously advised Roy to accept the mining man's proposal.

"I'll put you up a factory any place you say," said the millionaire, "and you can turn out all that we require. I've a notion, too, that they might be used as general freight carriers over arid stretches of country where there are no railroads, and feed and water for stock is scarce."

"Not a doubt of it," said Mr. Bancroft.

Before he left the preliminary papers had been drawn up and signed, and Roy Prescott found himself fairly launched in business. But in all this success he did not forget how much he owed to Peggy. Recent events had softened the boy's character and reduced his conceit wonderfully.

"I owe it all to you, little sis," he said that evening.

"I don't know about all," cried Jimsy, who was present; "but you do owe a whole lot to her, old man, and I'm glad to see you acknowledge it at last."

"I always have," cried Roy, turning rather red, though.

"Hum," commented Jimsy; "I'm not so sure about that."

But Peggy put her hand over his mouth and it took Jimsy what seemed an unduly long time to remove it. As for Jess, she stalwartly declared that if it hadn't been for Peggy there would have been no Golden Butterfly, no five thousand dollar prize, and, as she said, "no nothing." But to this loyal little Peggy would not assent. In her eyes Roy would always remain the most wonderful brother in the world.

Soon after this Jimsy and Jess took their leave and it was not long before the last light was extinguished in the happy little household and deep silence reigned. About midnight, as nearly as she could judge, Peggy awoke to find the moonlight streaming into her room and upon her face.

"Good gracious, I'll get moonstruck," she thought, and throwing on a wrap she went to the window to pull down the shade which had been raised to admit the cool air.

The window commanded a view of the workshop, in which the Golden Butterfly was kept, and Peggy, as she looked out, was astonished to see that the door of the work shop which housed the precious craft was open.

"Goodness!" thought the girl, "how careless of whoever left it that way. The night air will rust the stay-wires and the steel parts of the motor terribly. I guess I had better slip downstairs and close it."

Partially dressing herself the girl noiselessly tiptoed down the stairs and out into the moonlit night.

For one instant she was startled as she thought she saw a dark form dodge swiftly behind a corner of the workshop as she appeared.

"I must be getting as nervous as poor Roy when the mule frightened him down the well," she thought to herself as she advanced toward the shed. Reaching it she raised her hand to shut the door when, to her astonishment, she discovered that it had apparently been locked,—at least a broken bit of the padlock dangling from the portal seemed to indicate this.

"Somebody's filed that through," was Peggy's thought. But before she could make any further investigation a pair of hands grasped her from behind, pinioning her arms to her side. At the same instant an old coat was flung over her head and pulled close, stifling her outcries.

"We won't hurt you if you keep quiet," hissed a voice in her ear, "but if you don't, look out for trouble."

"What are you going to do?" cried Peggy, through the muffling medium of the coat.

"You'll soon find out," was the rejoinder. "Jukes, bring her inside the shed and keep her quiet."

Jukes! The name struck a familiar chord in Peggy's memory. She knew now why the face and form of the man hanging about Fanning's "Phantom" hangar at the aviation field had seemed so familiar to her. It was Jukes Dade, the man her father had peremptorily discharged. Peggy could not repress a shudder as she thought of the desperate character of the man.

Suddenly, as her captors half dragged, half carried her into the workshop, her body grew limp, and she fell in an insensible heap forward. She would have struck the ground had not a pair of hands caught her.

"She's fainted," cried Jukes, alarmedly.

"So much the better," growled out his companion; "she won't give us any trouble now. We can do what we've got to do and get away. Got the files?"

"Here they are," responded Jukes; "just let me lay her down here while I hand 'em to you."

He deposited Peggy's limp form on a long box on which some sacks had been strewn. The next instant the sharp rasping of a file could be heard in the silent workshop.

"I guess this Golden Butterfly will have its wings clipped for some time to come," chuckled Jukes' companion, whom Peggy, of course, had not yet seen.

"I guess that's right," laughed the other; "just wait a jiffy while I lay down this gun of mine and I'll give you a hand."

He stepped over and put down a wicked-looking pistol on the rough bench on which Peggy lay. Then he turned and began to help his companion. The two worked by the light of a dark lantern which they had brought with them on their rascally expedition to ruin the Golden Butterfly.

But suddenly a slight noise behind him made Jukes turn his head. As he did so he gave a startled yell. Peggy, her eyes bright and wild-looking, was standing up behind them. In her hand was the pistol which Jukes had laid down beside her when she had seemed to faint a few moments before. But Peggy's faint had been a simulated one. Realizing that harm was meant to the Golden Butterfly, she had imitated unconsciousness as a means to possible escape and giving the alarm.

"Don't move, either of you," said Peggy, in a firm voice. "I'm only a girl, but I can use a pistol."

But Jukes and his companion, with a wild yell, made a dash for the door.

"Good gracious, I can't shoot them," thought Peggy.

"Help! help!" she began to cry at the top of her voice.

But the next instant the whirr and roar of a motor from the road apprised her that the two rascals had made their escape in an auto and that pursuit was useless. Thus it was that when the aroused household came pouring excitedly out of the house they found a brave, if a rather tremulous, girl awaiting them with a pistol in her hand on the stock of which were engraved the initials "F. H."

"So that's who Jukes's companion was," exclaimed Roy, angrily. "Oh, if you had only awakened me, sis."

"My dear Roy," rejoined Peggy, with dignity, "don't you think that I am capable of taking care of myself?"

CHAPTER XXIV.
HESTER MAKES AMENDS—CONCLUSION.

A few days later Peggy borrowed Jess's car and went out for a long, lonely spin along the country roads. She wanted to think. Roy and Jimsy were at home repairing the damage wrought to the Golden Butterfly, which, it turned out, was very slight.

She was driving along a pretty stretch of road when she came across a veritable fairyland of delicate pink wild roses intertwined with honeysuckle and woodbine.

"Oh," cried Peggy, who simply worshipped flowers, "how beautiful; I must take some of these home. They'll make all our garden things look mean and shabby."

Stopping the car she alighted and was soon deep in her occupation of gathering the fragrant posies. Suddenly she was startled by the sound of a sobbing voice close at hand, and the next minute an angry male voice could be heard also.

"I tell you I'll do nothing of the sort," the man was saying; "why should I go and own up that I'm a thief or the next thing to it? At any rate they'd have me put in jail for all the attempts I've made to interfere with their aeroplane."

"It's Fanning Harding!" gasped Peggy, amazedly, "and Hester Gibbons," she added the next instant as the girl's voice sobbed out:

"Well, if you won't, I will. I've been weak and foolish but I'm not wicked. I'm going to tell Peggy Prescott all about it to-day and ask her to forgive me."

"You'd better not," Fanning Harding's tone was threatening now.

"Well, what if I do?"

"You won't, I tell you. I'll have you locked up and charged with the theft yourself."

"You wouldn't dare."

"Oh, yes, I would. You've got that ruby and that is pretty good proof that you stole it."

"It isn't so and you know it. I have been a weak, silly girl, that's all, but I see it all now. And just to think if I hadn't overheard you and my father talking that I might have gone on admiring you."

"Tell me you won't go to the Prescotts with the story or I'll—"

"Help! Help!"

The shrill cry came in Hester's tones.

Without quite realizing what she was doing, Peggy stooped and picked up a heavy bit of stick that lay in the road beside her. Then she stepped forward around a bend which had hitherto hidden the other two from her sight. As she appeared Fanning had his hand on Hester's wrist and was wrenching it cruelly.

"Oh! oh! Fanning, please let go!" Hester was crying.

"I will if you'll promise not to tell."

"There's no need for her to promise that, Fanning," said Peggy, "for I have already heard enough for me to know that she has some connection with the disappearance of the Bancroft diamonds."

"Oh, Peggy!" cried Hester, running to her side.

"See here," began Fanning, swaggering forward threateningly toward the two girls.

"My brother is just 'round that corner," said Peggy, boldly; "he'll be here in a minute. If you don't wish to be arrested for what you did the other night you had better get away from here, Fanning Harding."

A scared look crossed Fanning's face and he turned and fairly took to his heels.

"Now, Hester," said Peggy, kindly, "come with me to my car. It's just 'round the corner."

"Oh, Peggy, I've been a bad, wicked girl, but I'm not a thief. Truly I'm not."

"I believe that," said Peggy, "but what do you know about the disappearance of the diamonds?"

"That I have them all here. Not one is gone," was the amazing reply, and Hester, drawing a handkerchief from her bosom, unfolded it and displayed to Peggy's amazed eyes a glittering collection of gems. In the midst of the flashing gems gleamed the big ruby which Peggy had once seen Hester so carefully conceal.

"Hester, you have a duty before you," said Peggy slowly; "get in my car and come with me to my home and then tell me all about this mystery which has puzzled us so long."

But the girl shrank back.

"I can't. Oh, Peggy, with you it's different, but before, the others. Your brother—"

"Poor fellow, he has been under unjust suspicion on account of these very jewels," Peggy reminded the agitated girl.

"Oh, give me time. Not now. I—"

"No, it must be now," said Peggy, with gentle insistence. "Come!"

Something in her manner seemed to strike the girl.

"You'll promise no harm will come to me or my father through this?" she said.

"Is your father very deeply implicated in the matter?" asked Peggy seriously, looking straight into the other's eyes.

"No. On my word of honor, no," was the response.

"Then I'll promise," said Peggy.

"Very well, then, I'll tell you all I know about the matter," said Hester, as the girls got into the car.

An hour later, in the library of the Prescott's home, Peggy, Roy, Jimsy and Jess were gathered listening to Hester's story. Her eyes were red from crying and she hesitated frequently, but her manner showed that she was telling the truth.

On a table lay the glistening jewels. Jess had counted them and found that they were all there.

"I didn't find out about the jewels till one night Fanning, who has always said he admired me," said Hester, with downcast eyes, "gave me that big ruby there. At least he didn't give it to me but he said I could wear it. Of course I had heard about the disappearance of the jewels from the auto, but somehow I didn't associate this token of Fanning's with it.

"It was not till a week ago that I learned the true state of affairs. I overheard a conversation of Fanning's with my father in which he threatened him with arrest if he, father, didn't give him some money Fanning said he had hoarded up. I knew dad didn't have any and I asked him after Fanning had gone to tell me all about it.

"He isn't such a bad man at bottom and when I pleaded with him he told me the whole story. On the day of the jewel robbery, for it was a robbery, Morgan and Giles—"

"Our butler and groom!" cried Jess.

"Yes. Well, they were taking a stroll in the fields and happened along just as the car was wrecked. They knew from servants' gossip that you had been to town to get the gems and when they saw you lying unconscious and the wallet near at hand, the temptation was too much for them and they stole it.

"They determined to hide it in some woods near my father's place; but as they entered them Fanning Harding came along on his bicycle. He saw them enter the woods and became suspicious. Leaning his bicycle against a tree he followed them and saw them bury the gems under a tree which they marked.

"He noted the tree, too, and then, without their seeing him he remounted his motor-cycle and came on to see my father about that business of the hoax aeroplane. He said he wanted to bluff you into selling the Butterfly to him.

"Well, father agreed, for a fair sum of money, to help him, and we started right into town. At that time I thought it was a good joke, and we were both laughing as we came in sight of the scene of the accident."

"So that's what they were laughing at," thought Roy, recollecting how mystified he had been when he saw them together.

"I don't know whether it was Fanning's manner or what," said Hester resuming, "but my father began to suspect that he might know something about the jewels, and one day he followed him into the woods when he went to see if the jewels were still under the tree. Father made him own up when he caught him red-handed like that, but in the meantime Morgan and Giles also had arrived. Well, the four of them were all equally guilty, so they agreed to stick together and say nothing till the excitement about the loss had blown over. But

Fanning in the meantime said that he must have the ruby to let me wear.

"I guess he wanted to show me that he was as rich as he was always pretending to be.

"A few days later they had a terrible fright. Morgan, who carried the leather wallet in his pocket for lack of a better place to put it, dropped it on the porch of the Bancrofts' house where, as you know, it was found before he realized his loss and could recover it.

"When Fanning came back from the aviation meet and began boasting of the mean tricks he had played you and how he had kidnapped Roy, I began to see what a despicable fellow he was. Then, too, he was always threatening dad, and so I decided to make a clean breast of it all and save poor dad any more trouble, for Fanning has dictated to him ever since they shared the secret.

"I went to the wood and found the marked tree I had heard them talk about so often and with the jewels in my hand I started for your home, Peggy, for I didn't dare to go to the Bancrofts'. But Fanning, it seems, had got suspicious, and followed me. He overtook me at the spot where you encountered us."

"Does he know you have the jewels?" asked Roy.

"Not yet," rejoined Hester; "I believe if he had he would have been violent."

"Well, Hester," said Peggy, as the girl concluded her strange narrative, "you have cleared up a puzzling mystery."

"Did you ever hear such a yarn in all your born days?" asked Jimsy.

"And every one of the jewels is there," cried Jess. "I tell you what I'll do, I'll just call up the house and tell mother about it. Won't she be pleased?"

But Mrs. Bancroft was not at home, and—

"Oh, miss," gasped the servant, who answered the 'phone, "we're all upset. Morgan has run off, miss, and so has Giles. They took some of the silver with them. Mary and me tried to stop 'em but they pointed a pistol at us and scared us inter high strikes."

"I'll 'phone the police at once," cried Jess, indignantly. "They might have got off if it hadn't been for that."

But although a good description was furnished, Morgan and Giles were not captured and Mr. Bancroft was not ill pleased.

"They will not venture into this part of the country again," he said, "and we are well rid of such rascals."

Hester, in whom Mrs. Bancroft took an interest after the girl had told her with her own lips her strange story, is now at a girls' boarding school, having been sent there at Mrs. Bancroft's expense.

As for Fanning Harding, his father sent him West soon after the lad's innate rascality had been revealed, and from reports Fanning is working hard to redeem the past and make himself a good and useful man.

"And so the mystery of the phantom airship and the missing jewels is all cleared up," said Peggy to Jess one day a short time after the events just described had transpired.

"Yes," rejoined her chum, "and the air seems clearer and fresher somehow. It is terrible to have a dark cloud of suspicion hanging over one."

"It is, indeed," rejoined Peggy; "and now, as Roy leaves in a few days for the West, let's all take a good long spin. You and I will go in the Golden Butterfly while the boys can run along below us in the auto."

But Jess looked a bit doubtful.

"Wouldn't Roy like to go in the aeroplane?" she said.

Peggy broke into merry laughter.

"Oh, you sly puss," she exclaimed. "Very well, then you and Roy in the Golden Eagle and Jimsy and I in the auto."

"Suits me," cried Jimsy, throwing his arm around his sister's waist, "but I thought you were the girl aviator of the family, Peggy."

"So I am," laughed Peggy, "but I am willing to yield my place for once."

"Well, if you'll excuse my horrid slang," laughed Jimsy, "I think I may say we've all been 'up in the air' for the last few weeks. But it's all over now and we'll settle down to humdrum life once more."

"It's been jolly, though," protested Peggy.

"With some parts left out," put in Jess.

But although no adventures just like those we have related happened again to the Girl Aviators, they were due to encounter some more strange experiences. In fact, both Peggy and Roy and their friends were on the brink of some odd happenings, the narration of which must be postponed to another volume of this series.

What these complications and adventures, both merry and perilous, proved to be will be set down in full detail in "The Girl Aviators on Golden Wings," a breezy tale of our aerial maids.

THE END.